Global Warming − Social Story-Poems

SEEDS of NEEDS

The Urgency of Now in an Age of Change

General Design/Layout: Blue Light Series

Author: Martin Ray

Cover Design/Illustrator/Artist: Melanie Wichlein

Copyright: Blue Light Series 2016

Second Edition 2016

ISBN-13: 978-1523313945

ISBN-10: 1523313943

Other books in the Blue Light Series
Computer Comfort – (A modern approach to computer use)
Running Types (2016)

Global Warming - Time-Stories
If 'all the world's a stage', it's on fire. A Sense of Global Warming

Stories of Lala – Stories of Hope – Children's stories
Stories of Lala II – Creatures of the Forest (2016)

From 'The swing of the pendulum'

It was Rosa Luxemburg who said, if we do not go towards socialism we will turn to barbarism instead. A strange statement indeed but she saw something we need. If each thing has its own time and capitalism reaches the full end of its swing, then barbarism is what it will bring...

Don't we have any of this? (social changes)

Yes, we do, but social changes are small and often disconnected struggles. The struggles for all the previously mentioned ideas to bring about a more balanced society are happening now, somewhere. But it's like that famous old saying 'divide and conquer'. The rich and powerful controllers know this well. They divide, distract, and deflect attention with multiple methods; then social change stays only the dream, not the reality. Small successes are good and necessary stages, but that gives the illusion of change. The chess pieces are simply being moved around the table a little bit, the (deadly) game goes on.

CONTENTS

Introduction

It was recommended by Global Warming Awareness leaders, that it would be helpful through whatever medium of Art that people were interested in to raise awareness on this subject with the idea that anything that brings awareness is King. This is one of ours: story-poems and pictures to go.

All the short story-poems relate to Global Warming, **but in this project mainly to the social effects coming from the same connected causes.** Like many stories, there are problems, needs, and wishes, villains and Heroes. Some Heroes are in action and some are still a little sleepy. So it's also about the need for the Hero in us all to awaken and recognize not only the visible, but invisible chains of captivity that hold us back and down, and the need to release ourselves from these chains of oppression.

What do we need for the human race to survive? A livable planet seems to be first on the list. Another sane answer to that question would be to bring some form of democratic social balance to the world that would enable us to have a livable planet. It's a reasonable request, which of course would be an ideal and improved state for most people of our world.

Social justice, social balance, may seem unachievable in the struggle against the barriers placed in our way: due mostly to our attention, time, and energy being taken in the daily needs of survival in the societies that have developed.

We are told by many people these days the root cause of our varied social problems and also leading us to having a planet warming quicker than it should be - stem from the inherent inequality and systematic effects of our financial system, in a word, 'Capitalism'. Amazing, isn't it, all of our troubles can be summed up in this one word.

Why write another book on Global Warming Awareness and what can we hope to achieve, especially as we are not experts on the subject? It could be from anyone of you really, a mum, or dad, any concerned human.

Well, we are concerned humans and we have kids. I'm sure that when they are old enough, they too will want kids. And as it's clear for many, but not for all: our world, the one our kids will live in when we're dead, is Globally Warming. This will have all of the disaster effects that you may already know a bit about.

The Power of an Idea and of Wishing

There is inherent power in an idea, the idea of hope and of wishing; nothing comes without first the wish. So, like all the other writers on this subject, let's hope and wish for the 'butterfly effect'. You know the one: a butterfly flaps its wings one too many times somewhere and then comes a storm halfway around the world. You see the thing is, you don't really know which butterfly it was that caused that storm. And that storm may well be a hurricane.

It's the idea, the Image in picturesque form which contains a thousand connected ideas. That's what counts.

Imagine for a moment, that someone, anyone, anywhere, wrote or painted something inspiring others into actions, which in turn caused other people to lead the world to an age of change: to change the path our world is on. Now, any of those imaginary people could be any of you.

You might write those first words, write a song, join a movement, or start a movement. You might inspire some form of action, completely unaware. There's the 'butterfly effect' - in the human play of life. So dear reader, you're a butterfly, and this is the unfolding of the mystery of your life; with powerful wings of incipient change, strong enough even to alter the wind in other parts of the world. Butterflies are cool.

The Ocean of Our Emotion

The voice of this book simply joins into the many other voices, which quite frankly often get lost in the wilderness of our high speed world, like a drop in the ocean. But the ocean is made of many drops. And essentially it's the ocean of our emotions that we must navigate through - to eventually help and save our human family and any other beings that we can from the coming onslaught of climate changes.

Nothing except strong directed human emotion, personal and collective, will produce enough energy and impulse to affect and maintain a change in our social and world circumstance - in the time we need it most. This book is about this emotion.

We've been distracted for many years now from where we should be. And 'controllers of might', of power, are placing many distractions and blocks onto the path of change. The real problem is: time is running out. It's not that nothing is happening; there's lots happening: it's that we are simply running out of time. That and there are many barriers making change increasingly impossible - in the time we need it.

In regards to what would be possible for us in helping to stop our planet from so rapidly warming, until we try, we cannot tell what we can do. In order to change something one has to become aware enough of what the problem is. They say, history repeats itself, but only until there is no time left to repeat - which is the problem approaching us like a speeding train.

We have many needs, many demands; and there are many barriers. Social progress takes time to be seeded, and to bloom from the cultivation and care of those seeds of needs. Under any normal circumstances our needs would take time and a mass of collective simultaneous efforts.

Pandora's Box

Our circumstances are not normal. We are being delayed by multiple distractions; our attention is being deflected on many levels, from Media-Trivia, War, Starvation, Austerity Measures, and Survival, as well as embedding attitudes in people in general, which are negative or socially destructive to any chance of having a socially democratic society. There are many other negative effects that come with this Pandora's Box of tricks.

The main problem, to repeat, for it needs repeating: time runs out – hell, we don't even have a generation left. This is it, the fire's at the door, but the party's loud. The people enjoying the party, those in charge of it, in charge of all the food, the drinks, the entertainment, the security; they're having a ball. And they like to party, 24-7-365, they don't want to stop.

Perhaps if they did, they'd have to look at themselves, which as we all know, can be the hardest thing in the world: recognition in one's heart, of what one is oneself when alone, when no-one is looking. Often this may simply be a shallow person, a person of shallow being, made up of all the refinery of life, all that money can buy, but nothing that's real, no compassion or empathy for humankind in its potentially darkest hour.

As has been said by others before: it's world socialism or barbarism
that knocks on our door. As the planet heats civilization will collapse.
Time-wise it's not that far away. The darkest hour may not be here yet; but
many predict this to be the threat.

In charge of our world, there are powerful 'controllers of might'
with weak 'Being.' It was Plato who said,
'We need Teachers of Being.'
Unfortunately, this is the truth of what we are now seeing,
that has lead us to where we are now,
our leaders have had no 'Teachers of Being'.
So I suppose this is why we write,
just another voice on a dark night.

About the format

The prologue and epilogue have a purpose; they're not only for artistic pleasure. In the prologue you get two different sides of the same fence right at the beginning; two opposite points of view. It's the food for thought in the following pages which highlight more of the details. As to the epilogue, well, it's a little imaginative 'free license fun', that, and we like epilogues.

The intermission for 'questions and answers', 'good things and bad things', is a break. We tried to avoid sounding like the weatherman from hell, but due to the 'social commentary' needed for this particular project, you might need a break now and then anyway. Some themes overlap, common sense, social sense, simple common goodness, for they all relate to each other. They are connected threads that unfortunately wear a bit thin in our times. The story-poems weave in and out of these themes, trying to highlight that connectedness, or the lack of it.

The story-poems are written in slightly different styles, mainly to help make it different for you in reading. There is some sadness, not depression but sadness; as you will know, there is a big difference. We need rage and sorrow; the power of those emotions is justified in our circumstances. There's a touch of humour, but it's hard to make or include a little fun on the connected causes and effects of Global Warming; if one does, it begins to seem like sarcastic satire, which it's not meant to be, simply an effort to lighten the inherent load of this heaviest of themes.

The story-poems come in two categories, two voices so to speak. Sometimes there's a little bit of both in one story-poem; they intermix, just like in a real conversation. They are highlighted by the drawings at the top of the pages, a small picture of the world of the 99% and another of the 1%. But to a VIP (Very Interesting Point) - it's not actually the 1% of humanity that have this incredible wealth and power. Sure, they have enough, (it averages 2.7million for each person) but it's the 0.000001 percent, which are way too many zeros to have on each page.

So technically speaking, when we refer to the one percent, it's the 1 at the end of all those zeros before. (Of course in general, there are few people that wouldn't mind having more money, just to avoid eating cat-food at the end of their days.)

It doesn't really take that much money to be in the top one percent of earners in the world, due to the level of poverty of most. The problem is about the policies of the leaders of that world, which affect the real world - the one of the suffering.

Originally we were going to use a small drawing of a double decker bus that symbolically travels across the planet dropping off all the 'pleasures' of Pandora's Box on its path. To place that in half the pages throughout the book was a bit over the top. So we settled on something simpler. As to the bus: well, it's said that the richest 80-85 people in the world could fit on a double decker bus. Their riches averaging over 23 billion dollars each: which is as much as 3.5 billion of the bottom earners of humanity earn together.

As this book is mainly about the *cause and effect* of policies implemented by the one percent and suffered by the ninety nine percent, a double decker bus steam rolling over the world seems appropriate at least once.

VIP: Very Interesting Point

Right now, at the beginning, we will tell you an open secret which would help to assimilate the emotion necessary to generate that invisible quality people call energy, that passion that we so desperately need on a massive scale. So the open secret, what is it? It's your voice.

Words, their meanings and their sound, have an effect on the emotions. We all know this, it's why we are taken by songs so much. This is part of the idea of writing in poetic rhyme. If you have the possibility, read aloud, as if to others; not all the time, but sometimes. That has multiple benefits for you personally. Don't take our word for it, try it. It doesn't take long to recognize the power of your own voice developing. It will activate new connections in your brain; it will help you stay younger and more attentive. Although take speak-breaks; as you will know, information needs time to penetrate and deepen before meaning and understanding unfolds.

There are other benefits, but the main one is: as you speak, you will be affected more, it cuts closer to the bone. It brings your words and their meaning closer home.

If that's not enough, and you need further encouragement, well, added to that, on the social side of life, you will impress passers bye; start a conversation, make friends for life, fall in love, settle down, start a family, do social works for humanity together, save our planet - live happily ever after. You might sell more copies of this book for us, which will give us some money for other projects; or alternatively, we can invest in suntan lotion shares. Who knows? We're humans; our possibilities could be endless - if we had the time. Time is something we are running out of, so, wanna be a Hero of the modern world, in an Age of Change? If so, that would be great, our world needs you and needs you now.

Prologue

"Power concedes nothing without a demand" so what do we demand ?

As those who lead our planet towards climate destruction are the powerful in every land, remember that, "Power concedes nothing without a demand". What do we demand and what are we willing to endure? We know time's running out, that's for sure. An inter-connected matrix of power control, touch one string - it affects the whole. What do we demand? It's different in every land.

In some lands it will be cancelling the laws of Austerity that attack the poor to pay for the criminally rich and selfish who are beyond secure. In some countries, to stop privatizing seeds and buying up land that poor people need. In other places, racial and social justice for all - stop killing innocents just because they easily fall.

The ending of unnecessary unemployment, creating a planetary workforce for saving our only planet, meaningful work – damn it. Creating laws for free health care for everyone, everywhere, is where our taxes should be spent; it's where we thought they were going, to our betterment.

With all the money spent on War and our children dying and they don't know what for, demanding an end to War is a human practicality. War brings nothing but what we already know. Ceasing the invasion of other lands to increase the profits of corporate brands should be high on the list of all these demands. Demands, these should be indeed, we have a planet burning and humankind in need.

Not all demands will be achieved, but the ball is rolling – if it stops, a hot planet we bequeath. The call is clear: it's time for change; it's been held just out of range, we got distracted a while back, Wars and Austerity Measures two ways but on one track.

"Occupy the public; give them stuff to do,
tell them it will all be better soon,
in a few months, maybe next June.
Delay, distract, divert attention away,
it's their 'goldfish attention', we trained them that way."
We have demands that must be met,
if 'they' don't give, we don't get,
but we've been distracted in the fights for our common rights,
in every land in different ways,
'suffer the poor', is the only thing that's for sure.

Money talks and money walks and flies, there's no boundaries, no borders, no control, for those who sold our planet, human rights and their soul, so the rich get richer every day. In general our demands are local, and affect our own, but where is the key that unlocks it all? Many say: it's capitalism that has to fall. That of course returns our world to a different state, and if power concedes nothing, we have a long wait. Humans struggle now for a long time; we've endured a lot for a humanity to find, sold down the drain of pain, time and time again.

We demand places of care for the old or the homeless.
We demand safety for women to walk in the street.
We demand that violence they do not meet.
So we must demand an education that considers this in all lands,
for what we demand takes time to understand
and needs time to penetrate into the soul of man.
But we demand it begin now, education free for all,
we demand this first of all.

We demand more money for our work; we demand equal pay for all.
Do we demand too much? No, not at all.
Within the last hundred years it could have went this way,
but we travelled on a different path.
Where capitalism leads, has an aftermath.

We demand no more oil to be found.
We demand the oil to be left in the ground.
That's a fight but it should be our human right.
So we demand the right to protest the unjust,
this demand is a must.

We demand that there be no secret laws,
we demand the powerful to be held to account.

We demand and must see all governments' transparency.
We demand that those who speak about broken laws should be
welcomed for this cause.
Do we demand too much? No, we demand not enough.
Do we demand cake to eat?
No, we demand bread and shoes for our kids' feet.

We demand a planet free from company crime.
We demand a change in laws.
We demand to be free from their destructive claws.
We, the poor, in every land have our own different demands,
so what is it to be - revolution or reform?
How do we get to where real humanity should be the norm?
Do we protest and the battlements storm?
Or possibly even better, do we refuse to shop and buy,
do we boycott companies that lie, can our demands be heard?

Are we clear about what we demand, can our voice be loud enough to command –
a change? Our demands are many, but so are we. We call the powerful to
accountability, for they placed themselves at the top of the hill; controlling the poor
seems to be a thrill. Being-less leaders have the normal weaknesses of men; they
weaken time and again, weaken to the fact that power corrupts.

Remember, remember - this is no gunpowder plot.
The poor are simply the people the rich forgot.
Many reasons can be said, but our planet heats,
it's time for new laws to be read, capitalism is a lonely bed.
We demand a new social justice,
new laws from all governments to pass;
this is a demand from the poor who should command
through a common social sense, for we need leaders who cannot be bought.
We demand a change in the chain of command.
We demand a media, beholden to the people,
for social common human laws, one voice one cause.

We demand to be free of nuclear war
where darkness would fill our sky.
We demand leaders with a developed sense of being,
and not leaders who only enjoy themselves seeing.

We demand a lot, but do we? I think not.
Normal human demands in any land,
it's only those in power that will concede nothing without a demand.
There's a little cosmetic 'give and take',
but they keep their control well in hand.

What we demand should have been common rights by now,
we demand a world of peace, we demand all wars should cease,
we demand the hungry to be fed,
we demand the homeless to have a bed,
we demand that you stop droning us from the sky,
oh, we understand why.
'Control the land, control the oil, control all the fertile soil,
kill the poor, make them bleed, then what we sell they will need.'

Well, we demand a life. We demand equality to people of all colours. We demand all religions to be recognized for we are the 99% of humankind, and this world is ours and this is not a request, these are our demands, and we hope you understand, for they will change as time goes by. The less you do for us now, the more we will try and the more we will demand. Dear powerful and rich, one day, you will understand.

We are the powerful in control.

Here's what we demand for it to stay so

We demand you fall down and accept
all the injustices that into your life have crept.
We demand our media that we control
to divert you with meaningless trivia shows.
We demand all natural resources to be taken from earth and used.
We demand the world to abuse.

We demand to be left in peace.
We demand your protests to cease.
We don't demand too much.
We don't need to, we manipulate it, it's your crutch.

It's embedded in your education, what little we let you have,
and it will stay that way without cessation.
Unconsciously you will comply with what we demand;
embedded communication is what we understand.
We demand and we will keep our system in which we all the profits reap,
and reap we do, it's nothing new,
it's been that way all time through, we think it's pretty fine,
'All for us and none for you', we demand you think this too.

We demand the power to control,
all politicians to stop you from becoming an organized whole.
We know that you are a mass and a power to behold,
so we keep you worried and separate, you'll do what you're told.
We manipulate and demand
that you'll hate others not of your colour brand.

We vilify and destroy any hope of unity with a new toy,
a film, a game, an article of news.
We demand that you think other religions to abuse.
We demand that you be sent to war,
and we manipulate it so that you do not really understand what for.
For justice, for safety, for anything you like,
we give you lots of reasons; our media is the drink we spike.

We demand that you worry about survival every day.
We demand that you accept low pay.
We demand that our companies have human rights.
We demand that you accept that our day is your night.
We demand that you do not care about what we do to others – over there –
people of another colour or religion or race.
We demand and manipulate that you don't see
that they too have a human face.

****

We demand that you watch films that help and make you understand,
that what we do in your name is good for you and yours,
so feel no shame. We feel no shame at all in what we demand from all,
submission to our cause - hell, we write these laws.
We demand and make it so
that into your life we get to know - everything about you
and that information will serve us well,
this you know; this you can tell.
Now we've fixed it in the system, it's under our control,
you will never be free, you will never be whole,
we will keep you well apart; freedom is a dying Art.

We demand of you to accept to live in Austerity, and deep in debt,
and we still demand that you buy all our stuff,
you can never have enough.
We demand you pay for health care, we demand you pay for
all you got. We demand if you're black - accept being shot.
This is how we keep control, this is how you will never be whole;
this is how we make you hate each other so.

Your minds are easy for us to manipulate, you the poor had a few decades where
you thought freedom and the good life was at the gate. But we were working in the
dark; our seeds of horror became a spark that started to flame
and fire out of your control.
We seized the world, now you know.
We ride the dragon that does prevail.
We breathe fire and destruction, we cannot fail.

****

We demand from our 'media minds' to manipulate you and for you to buy all you
do: as to your money, well, yes, that came to us
we have that now, but with your mind we left you blind
and fighting down below, distracted and deflected your attention away, so you don't
see the destruction we bring.
We had a song we made you sing.
Disaster we have mastered, it brings us money too,
you send it all on to us this we thought you knew,
sure, a little gets to those broken lands,
but they're so far away that you don't really understand.

And we pretend that we do care, we make tax exempt charities for you down there,
and perhaps we do, some of us, deep inside,
but we find our system of capitalism is a lovely ride.
With all the money floating to the top, well, it's just like all the oil in the ocean,
it begins to drop and contaminate and destroy all life down below,
it's darkness seeping into every living thing.
You're an externality and your planet is too.
We didn't realize that this is what we do,
but now we know, and so do you.
That's just how life is - accept it - we do.

Do you think we will reform? Not likely.
Do you think your protests affect us? Not really.
Do you think our politicians are not paid well enough?
Do you think we don't have enough security?
Do you think we trashed your education for no reason?

We're addicted to power; do you think your protests are rehab?
Do you think anything you say can change our ways?
Do you really think a revolution would work?
Do you think the police everywhere in every country have been militarized for fun?
Do you think you can survive under a warming sun?
Do you think you can speak to power or do you think you should run?
Do you think there's anywhere you can hide?
Do you have the latest phone, because if you do,
you're never alone?

We will hold you down in chains, many are invisible, but we hold the reigns, we guide and we control, we demand that you are never an organized whole. We ride the wave upon the sea of life. We control your destiny. Our demands are really simple – in the end. We demand you do what we say. We are your masters and we rule you night and day. We demand that you have nothing real, we like it that way. This is what we demand, and we will force you to understand. You can struggle and even fight, but remember, remember, we are the 'Masters of Might'.

Seeds of Needs

The Urgency of Now - in an Age of Change

Who are the Heroes of Today?

Who are the Heroes of today? Some are those who break the silence
and speak up and say – this is wrong.
Some of them try to lead us back to where we belong.

Who are the Heroes of today? Those mums who must fight austerity
measures and work for little pay,
they try to struggle through this inhuman way.

Who are the Heroes of today? Some of them take to the streets and
raise their voice and say,
this is unjust; human rights are a must.
They gather in their thousands now, everywhere,
they know they are not alone, they fight for human rights.
The silent herd are silent no more, at the moment it's a rumble;
it will gather force until it becomes a roar.

Who are the Heroes of today? Some sing songs, it's their way.
To sing a song of protest is not despair,
the sound of the human voice is always heard out there.

****

Who are the Heroes of today? Many are in lands far away;
they struggle to survive - just one more day,
to make it through the night, to hold their children tight,
waiting for that bomb to drop, waiting for the bullets to stop.
Children raised in fear of sound, of a drone flying all around.
Even just to step outside into the freshness of the day,
makes you a Hero if you live that way.

When your home is ripped apart, this is not a human art,
and you begin again to build, brick for brick, stone for stone,
there's something inside you; it's a Hero that is never alone.
Simply to continue day after day and hope things get better in some way,
then you have the heart of a Hero in you,
for there are so many that could not continue.

Who are the Heroes of today? There are so many in every land
that are oppressed, there are so many that others do detest.
Have they been educated to be that way, brought up and raised to be a bigot,
a racist, in words or silently, taught by example to live a lie,
that I am better and it's others that should die?

Is that a sacred thing, what the young are taught to sing,
to hate others of another faith, a colour, a race, to spit in their face, and only love
their own? Just to still walk around in the street with so much hate coming at them,
makes a Hero that you don't see. The Hero lies in their heart invisibly.

How much hate can people endure,
it would test the patience of an angel, that's for sure.
Yes, men do fear for their life,
but mainly it's for their children or their wife.

****

Who are the Heroes of today? Those who go to gather wood
and make small talk, many must watch where they tread,
for a buried landmine will be their bed.
And usually it's kids or women that get blown apart,
land mines – a modern art.

****

Who are the Heroes of today? The old man and woman who only
have enough money to eat cat-food:
as they sit with fork in hand it doesn't take much to understand,
that as that fork moves slowly to those lips,
there's a Hero in those fingertips,
a Hero who wants to live, that refuses to roll over and simply die,
from forced austerity measures from 'the rich' up high.

It's obviously not hard for the rich to go to bed at night and sleep,
knowing that the old, the poor, the unfed have no decent food, home or bed,
all because the money went to their head.

And they cry for more laws to make
for the Heroes of the poor, they try to kill or break.
Shame on those who are the extreme rich,
they have no hero, just an itch.

****

Who are the Heroes of today? The Hero lies within us all
and it's a silent inner call.
In different lands it's different pressure,
different struggles seize the day.
It's hard to empathize with other people's way.
So who are the Heroes of today?
They are many, too many to say,
but they're a Hero in their own way.

Part Two

Today

Who's responsible for the poor that live in our concrete cities of camps of pain? Who owns that land, who gains? And who are the Heroes that must live there, day after day, year after year. Bring up a family, struggle just to survive, to live this inhuman way; instead of thrive. To choose between heat for the home and food for the kids, that young mum makes a Hero's choice, day by day.

Who is responsible for the policies of pain that send women, children and the old to live in squalor, tarpaulin tents, to die of cold or hunger? Who's responsible for those policies of planetary care? Who's responsible for putting them there? They are heroes but their fates were sold. Sure, we say wars of conquest or austerity has victims, it happens all through time. It's the constant policy from those who don't mind. Nothing touches those leaders who have no sense of better being; this is something that we're always seeing.

To live in desperation or despair, to never have a home again, anywhere; those people who live in refuge in many lands with only tents, just to struggle to stay alive, suffer much that others do not and cannot understand, if you don't live there in their land. We thank our God it's not us, but the weather's changing, what goes around, comes around. What swings one way swings back one day.

One day

They are Heroes that protest for peace. They are heroes that go to prison for drones to cease. They are Heroes that simply fight for normal human rights, and they are Heroes that sleep in the frozen cold streets at night; that suffer from a society that has been their unmaking, an unbalanced system, its people forsaking. There are so many Heroes in all our lands, it's impossible to comprehend or understand.

Heroes wrapped in news-papers in the street, who freeze night after night and a cold lonely end they meet, they are Heroes of our human race; they struggle despite their social place; to stay alive, to survive another day. This person was a child and loved sometimes, all and any sorts of horrors can lead us to this end, falling off the social structure, that's a state difficult to mend. To be a bag lady of the street, to beg for money off strangers you meet, to be an untouchable, never to be loved again, to have no-one, not one single friend, what a fate, at the end: and every time we turn and look away, we ourselves die a little every day.

There's a Hero in us all, the Hero's waiting for you to listen to the call, its almost silent whisper a caress, it's like a feather that strokes your heart. You and the Hero can never part, you can ignore the Hero in you, this is true, many do, one day you will turn and see, that this is how you were meant to be: to be a Hero to us all.

24-7-365

24-7-365 24-7-365 24-7-365 24-7-365 24-7-365 24-7-365 24-7-365
24-7-365 24-7-365 24-7-365 24-7-365 24-7-365 24-7-365 24-7-365
24-7-365 24-7-365 24-7-365 24-7-365 24-7-365 24-7-365 24-7-365
24-7-365 24-7-365 24-7-365 24-7-365 24-7-365 24-7-365 24-7-365
24-7-365 24-7-365 24-7-365 24-7-365 24-7-365 24-7-365 24-7-365
24-7-365 24-7-365 24-7-365 24-7-365 24-7-365 24-7-365 24-7-365
24-7-365 24-7-365 24-7-365 24-7-365 24-7-365 24-7-365 24-7-365
24-7-365 24-7-365 24-7-365 24-7-365 24-7-365 24-7-365 24-7-365
24-7-365 24-7-365 24-7-365 24-7-365 24-7-365 24-7-365 24-7-365
24-7-365 24-7-365 24-7-365 24-7-365 24-7-365 24-7-365 24-7-365
24-7-365 24-7-365 24-7-365 24-7-365 24-7-365 24-7-365 24-7-365
24-7-365 24-7-365 24-7-365 24-7-365 24-7-365 24-7-365 24-7-365
24-7-365 24-7-365 24-7-365 24-7-365 24-7-365 24-7-365 24-7-365
24-7-365 24-7-365 24-7-365 24-7-365 24-7-365 24-7-365 24-7-365
24-7-365 24-7-365 24-7-365 24-7-365 24-7-365 24-7-365 24-7-365
24-7-365 24-7-365 24-7-365 24-7-365 24-7-365 24-7-365 24-7-365
24-7-365 24-7-365 24-7-365 24-7-365 24-7-365 24-7-365 24-7-365
24-7-365 24-7-365 24-7-365 24-7-365 24-7-365 24-7-365 24-7-365
24-7-365 24-7-365 24-7-365 24-7-365 24-7-365 24-7-365 24-7-365
24-7-365 24-7-365 24-7-365 24-7-365 24-7-365 24-7-365 24-7-365
24-7-365 24-7-365 24-7-365 24-7-365 24-7-365 24-7-365 24-7-365
24-7-365 24-7-365 24-7-365 24-7-365 24-7-365 24-7-365 24-7-365
24-7-365 24-7-365 24-7-365 24-7-365 24-7-365 24-7-365 24-7-365
24-7-365 24-7-365 24-7-365 24-7-365 24-7-365 24-7-365 24-7-365
24-7-365 24-7-365 24-7-365 24-7-365 24-7-365 24-7-365 24-7-365
24-7-365 24-7-365 24-7-365 24-7-365 24-7-365 24-7-365 24-7-365
24-7-365 24-7-365 24-7-365 24-7-365 24-7-365 24-7-365 24-7-365
24-7-365 24-7-365 24-7-365 24-7-365 24-7-365 24-7-365 24-7-365
24-7-365 24-7-365 24-7-365 24-7-365 24-7-365 24-7-365 24-7-365
24-7-365 24-7-365 24-7-365 24-7-365 24-7-365 24-7-365 24-7-365
24-7-365 24-7-365 24-7-365 24-7-365 24-7-365 24-7-365 24-7-365
24-7-365 24-7-365 24-7-365 24-7-365 24-7-365 24-7-365 24-7-365
24-7-365 24-7-365 24-7-365 24-7-365 24-7-365 24-7-365 24-7-365
24-7-365 24-7-365 24-7-365 24-7-365 24-7-365 24-7-365 24-7-365
24-7-365 24-7-365 24-7-365 24-7-365 24-7-365 24-7-365 24-7-365
24-7-365 24-7-365 24-7-365 24-7-365 24-7-365 24-7-365 24-7-365

Rich Words – 24-7-365

Young mothers turned out into the street
as money travels upwards for the rich to meet.
Bankers play monopoly with people's lives,
they always have a 'get out of jail free card.'

The rich see protests and have them barred.
They don't care the people are starved.
Starved, not only of food, compassion and empathy would be good.
The poor must find a doorway to sleep the night through,
under a bridge, high on a girder - sometimes that will do.
It's not safe to live this way,
but it's what you must do, the rich do say.

****

You are the common of our land, you should by now understand,
that what you have can be taken from you,
as for us - that's what we do.
It's built in our system to be this way,
predatory capitalism rules today,
and we will play you to comply,
24-7-365 media keeps the lie.

******

You're occupied, it's a word we like, it's in all the drinks that we spike.
Fight for your freedoms - it's what you should do.
Of course we'll ignore you for a while,
we'll reply with a sympathy smile,
but if you're loud enough and make some noise,
you'll get our attention and we'll give you nice toys,
a new phone with a real cool app
just so we know where you are, on any map.

Protest and get violent if you will,
let's hope you have the money for the hospital bill,
because even that these days we make you pay,
someone has to for spoiling our day.

Non-violent protest - that's cool too,
sometimes we let you do what you want to do,
we can work it so some of you will rage,
this is our play - we set the stage,
and we will promise you many a thing,
because it takes a while to see what those promises bring.
And by the time that you realize all we did,
you'll be occupied with something else we hid.
It could be war in other lands - that you don't want,
but we'll convince you that you do,
we'll tell you; 'otherwise it will come home to you.'

We'll send your children off to war;
after all, you need something to die for.
If that's not enough and you still protest, (and spoil our day)
austerity measures usually works best.
They'll make you struggle to survive;
give you little work for little money, there's no-way you will thrive.
You will struggle to make ends meet;
protest away, it's a dead-end street.

****

These days we are well protected,
distractive selected media leaves our work undetected,
so we can go about our day.
Of course sometimes you get in our way,
but not enough to spoil our game.
We have no compassion, empathy or shame.
And funnily enough, we do all this in your name.

****

Each and every one of you would love to live the life we have,
we embedded it in your education long ago, when you were young,
so you sing the song that we want sung.
You want fame, you want riches, it's much the same, we give you TV ads that are
directed towards people with just your name.

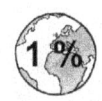

We have all and it stays that way, you get less every day,
and now, you will all struggle to survive, as your planet burns all alive.
That time will be upon all our kids,
but ours will have air conditioning,
yours will be in the row called skids.

Poverty comes to most my friend, but at night when you sleep in the street,
at least the weather will be a treat, a warming end it will be.
To us this is clear, but it's something you don't see.
Thanks to you we had a ball, we really enjoyed it all,
someone had to pay, it might as well be you,
'All for us and none for you'.
It's a motto that for us is always true.

Common Goodness

There is a common goodness to be found,
it lies in most people, it's all around.
It's there with so many people you meet in the street,
it's not about some higher being to meet,
it's in the care we show to other beings as through life we go.
From the controllers in power, it's not goodness that they show.
That goodness that lies in all within
in the 'Controllers Of Might': it's covered over, that's a sin.
There must be something that knows deep inside,
but from the common people their goodness does hide.
So it's not about some higher being,
it's about a common thing that we should be seeing.

*******.

There is evil in this world, this is obviously true,
although most people do not think that evil they do,
but if your actions make others sad,
and lead to despair,
and this you know, then your conscience fell down below.
Simple common goodness is a necessary stage,
if you want to stop the fire of your actions from the rage.
And rage like a fire out of control;
it will never leave you alone or leave you whole.

When people die from your wars then you have no just cause.
Your wars of control over oil
are a sad act, when these days it should be left in the soil
and Mother Earth intact.

Wars of austerity on the poor treat humankind like manure,
so much sadness and hardship is caused by you
and those actions that you do.

When you underpay the working class or keep them unemployed,
these are actions that you have enjoyed.
When you outsource work to other lands
and force the poor to endure, there is no-one who understands.

When you militarize the police, the protectors of our streets,
then you're waiting on the blowback of your selfish deeds
and unfortunately that will come.
Being-less leaders at the end you will have no friends,
no place to hide, no place to go
because if all the world's a stage, then on Earth,
it will become the hottest show.

Your common goodness took a walk,
no, that's a mistake, it ran in shock.
At the pleasure in the soul-less acts you take,
common goodness was burned at the stake.

Beast of Prey

The mask is on, the fire's alight,
the people claim a voice on this dark night.
The dark night of the human soul;
where humanity tries to be one whole.
But it's difficult to find a path, if all you do incurs their wrath,
and they have many ways to silence dissent.
There is no way they will repent, their path is never straight,
it's always a little bent.

They give you other worries to occupy your day,
there's no time to consider what our scientists say,
that the world is warming faster than we can control.
We're heating up our earth and losing all species whole.
But now, the people claim a voice, in who leads us, we have a choice.
Democracy, just another money making trick.
'Keep people poor; make them pay even when they're sick.
Turn out people in the streets to survive on scrapes and bits of anything that they
can find, the poor, they are the blind.'

But we have a voice, we have a choice,
each and every one a 'Hero' can become, it's something that we all need
or the 99 will only bleed.
Our children will die many types of death.
They kill our education and kick us when we're down.
They don't mind if we fight and struggle with each other,
or another race. A different colour is always good;
it keeps the poor from complaining "we have no food."

'We give them reasons and give them toys to play,
and they must pay more every day.'
People fall down dead and all alone in the street,
a cardboard box end they meet,
or bodies burned into the sky, the rich won't pay for the poor,
'A box for them! No, they'll be manure.'

A hundred years of betterment gone in the twinkling of an eye.
The rich have organized their laws and hold us in their claws
and claws it is indeed,
for they are the 'Beast of prey' that we are taught to heed.
Their policies have been embedded,
they seem separate but they are threaded,
and it's a web of manipulated deceit,
so that all people will poverty meet.
There's no way for humans to survive,
if they do not struggle to be alive.
Their human rights have been trashed and shred,
poverty is a lying and dying bed.

****

'Control the herd and let them think they are free;
tell them how they live is democracy.
Now we know it's not and it's just a game, we're the super-rich
and feel no shame, we rigged the rules, this is our game.
Enjoy the reality T.V. show, there's a lot on the box,
but you live the one you know.
We control the companies that give you mental satisfaction.
It's a really cool distraction.
You will sit night after night, year after year,
until we've taken all you hold dear.
So enjoy your reality T.V. show,
for your reality is the only one you'll ever know.

We even tell you what's in store,
we give you films that make us billions by the score.
With the pretty people we pay very well,
it's the media blitz that we sell.
Our scriptwriters write till late at night, so you in your day dreams want to be just
like them, rich and famous.
Now of course they are rich, we keep it that way
but they don't control the policy we sell,
we do - and that you knew.

We trash the planet and yes it's such a shame,
but the rules are fixed we can't change our destructive game.
The game is fixed until the end
unless a revolution is around the bend.

For that we have eyes and ears everywhere,
we pay them well, so for us they will care.
It's built into the system that rules your every day.
You may live in modern times but you'll never have a say,
so enjoy your reality T.V. show it's the only one you'll ever know.

The poor stay poor, the rich enjoy what riches bring. The world heats, the poor die
a poor death; we squeeze them till their last breath.
We like it that way, where we have the say.
We have plans in the making, the poor we must be forsaking.
People struggle to stay alive,
we like it like that for we need workers for our hive.
We let you breed, for your bodies we have a need.
Through lack of real food you will drop like flies,
but slowly the planet heats and burns everything alive.
Us too in the end, but we'll survive a little bit longer,
technology is our friend, when you can afford it.

****

As time goes by, we the super-rich will build cities in the sky
but not only, in mountains we will cut a city of marble where we will strut,
air conditioned of course to a tee, we will live selfishly,
and you the poor will build them for us.
We'll tell you, you can live there too,
but it's just a 'razz', a story, a tale, we'll tell to you,
it's your future, you cannot fail.
You must work and build to stay alive, for the sake of humanity,
you see with a heating world we must do all we can, but you can't blame us the
super-rich, you must blame the common man.
Another race, another colour, another religion is always good to blame;
it keeps you from looking at us and seeing our unholy shame.
Of course shame is something we have not,
it's like everything it can be bought.'

A Bridge of Inspiration!

Not really, more like a bridge of desperation and death

I read some poetry about a bridge the other day.
Some tried to copy Shakespeare's way,
some paid due to Mr Wordsworth and how and what he did say
and yet others did depart – new ways for a dying Art.
The beauty and the obviousness were all there
and sometimes that bridge's history;
even the mundane came in and took a chair.

There was a line maybe two that brought it to the bridge anew,
many wrote about times past, as well about the greatness of empire.
Sadly, no words were to be directly read about the causes of the poverty
that led too many to make that bridge their bed.

In the day many drive over the top, but in the night under is where they stop
to rest and sleep away the trouble of their economic woes,
that 'oh so romantic bridge', their metal bed and home, God knows.

The drugged, the drunk, the dying, the lonely, the depressed, the homeless,
the untouchables of our society find many a bridge their noisy home.
When a cold wind blows, you're alone.

Slid into the life of the modern disposable human waste,
who knows the fate of individual men – what they once were –
or even could be again, - if only - the tide of misfortune could change its wind.

Throughout our world today,
imposed austerity measures guides this play.
Break down the poor, starve them out, truth be told of what I behold,
I find no beauty in their bridge;
I passed there in my youth and walked hand in hand at night,
a romantic moment in soft moonlight,
but your senses must be limited so,
if you're not aware of life down below, the life that doesn't really live.
So no, I find no beauty in this bridge.

This is a metal house for homeless on the river's edge,
where the homeless must sleep back to back
and high on the girders for fear from attack,
with the politicians of our government causing more people to lose
their 'home sweet home'.
Condemned forever our cities' streets to roam,
no, there's no beauty in that.

****

As life does pass on bye, if you could hear your heart it would cry,
for that person you just passed is someone's child, alone at last.
So tie yourself to your mast
and thank your God your time has not yet passed.
One day you may truly be
that "Man in the mirror" that you so wish to see.
Connecting in, connecting out, connecting to a bridge of doubt,
I sense myself.

So on with the story as the story goes and 'dear readers' to calm you down
and not make you frown
but touch your heart to think and your lips, truth to drink.
As you cross or gaze upon a bridge,
some days you may not just get lost in its beauty.
It may remind you of the slave-built glutinous empire of our inglorious and violent
past and of that we only have a mast...
a bridge at last.

****

All we have has been bought
with blood, sweat, tears, and fears,
leading to a world where most of the population now live in arrears.
Dark things lie or work in the dark,
while the homeless try to sleep in the park.
A 'commons' it is no more, for that gets locked and there is no door.
The homeless that are all around,
have sweet bridges that they found,
when everything is under lock and key,
and borders block land and sea,
and cameras film you everywhere you go,
future street lighting seemingly, will be the 'Reality' TV shows.

Phones are made on the cheap, so everyone has a built in 'beep'
to listen into what you say or think and like a vampire take a drink, from the
thoughts that go through your mind, it feeds their flame which is a fire and it
consumes all that we the 'public' desire.

Which might be just simple but threatening in their way,
freedom, food, water, democracy, choice,
and to live in peace and have a voice.
One that may be humanly respected
not just heard because it was detected.
There'll be nothing secret that you can keep
even if you lay under a bridge to sleep.

And there's no money to buy some bread
and your children are dying, if not dead;
just remember these words in your heart and head.

'We do this all for you in order to protect,
and all the things we know that you do not suspect,
we can tell you what is good
even if austerity leaves you with no food.
Investments we will make for you
and in some things we have to choose
for we cannot let our markets lose.

The choice is a simple one to make,
no bread for you, 'try some cake'.
Oh, and by the way, Global Warming, that's a fake,
it's not real, trust us, we've made a deal.'
Pretend from Heaven's globe you could see,
there a question may be asked of thee,
with what you knew, what on Earth did you do?

****

Part Two

Look, see, sense, and shame, a bridge built in your name.
'Look at all those bridges built for you, well, in reality it's to make things easier and kept on the move, so that the businesses of our society we can improve. And yes, we know some of you sleep under there at night, it's a lovely view of the moonlight, as it glitters upon the passing water which runs dark and deep, and if you're not careful, when you roll over, those waters will you keep.

Equality for humans, that's just a myth, a fairy tale, a story to be told, to keep your hope a little bold. As you gaze truly through times past you see the horrors of our world come here to rest at last. We have a society now that can never be free, we have rules and regulations – hell – we have Austerity.

We make the poor pay for what we do, if you don't manage, we take your house away from you. Down the social structure you will fall, we don't really mind, we have too many of you all. So - yes - of course, you will sleep where you can, you are what we have created, the common man. Enjoy your bridge; these are the results of our Austerity, on that you can depend, this is what many of you will meet and cat-food will be your friend.

Our rules are fixed, money travels upwards in space, it goes against gravity, but we own this place, so we can do what we want and we do so all the time, and when we break the law there's no way it's a crime. We don't punish each other, that's not our way, you should by now the laws of Austerity understand, we have them in every land.

Now you can protest all you wish; we'll just cook up another dish, we can change the style and change the name for a while, hell – we'll distract you with another war, give you lots of reasons to send your kids off to die, we'll make sure that you don't know it's a lie, but if our deception you do detect, that's okay – we'll give you minorities to suspect.

Any will do, we just divide, distract, and destroy any social movement, even with a simple new toy. After all we own what you enjoy. And we embed it in your education and your every thought, everything you want must be bought, and you will pay with blood, sweat, and tears, in the end you will be in arrears. Then you will borrow from us and be in debt, 'that's nice'. You're just our human pet.

We are the captains of this ship, we're on a luxury cruise and it's a long trip, but we have lots of bridges that we built in the past and at your end they'll be your home at last.

But first, a word to let you know for evil always tells where it will go. Eventually we will pass laws and rules that we won't put up with homeless fools. It will become illegal to sleep under a bridge or in the street, there will be no commons for the homeless to meet, no cardboard cities either in the end, for on our price of property we do depend. We don't want you to spoil our day, not when we can lock you all away.

Being homeless will be a crime, so we will put you under lock and key, it makes no difference what colour or nationality. We build and privatise our prisons now; we plan for the future – funny – we thought you knew that too. Enjoy the bridges while it lasts, pretty soon even that will pass.'

Do you want to be loved? Buy this and you will be.

Simplify IT - Buy IT

FOR REAL MEN

BUY IT NOW BEFORE IT IS OUTDATED

FOR SALE: useless, current, unpayable stuff

don´t wait, don´t hesitate, now is the best time.

Everything on sale even a Whale !

GET A NEW LIFE BUY THIS NOW!

AMAZING OFFERS! It's impossible to say no.

IT´S JUST 4U

LIVE FOR 2DAY BUY NOW

Buy it, as long as you can!

What are you waiting for? Soon it will be too late!

BUY ! BUY ! BUY !

MADE BY THEIR KIDS FOR YOUR KIDS

If you have one you will be envied by all.

Feel It Try It Buy It

The best for the best.

nothing for the rest.

Try Me Buy Me

This can change your life.

Money is not the most important

thing, so why don´t you spend it all?

BUY NOW PAY LATER

IT LASTS FOREVER 2 Year Guarantee

BUY ! BUY ! BUY !

Buy what makes you happy!

FOR SALE

Wear this suit and show who you really are!

We Feed your needs

BUY ! BUY ! BUY !

Boys, if this you buy, girls won´t walk by !

MADE 4U

GET THE LATEST MUST-HAVE HERE

MADE BY CHILDRENS HANDS

Buy 3 for 2! (Even if you don´t need it)

BUY THIS! You will never regret it.

don´t miss this opportunity

AVALEBLE ONLY

The Consumer Plot

The 'consumer plot', once you're born, you're bought

'We have not yet reached our peak,
for we don't have all yet that we seek,
we have a still expanding all encompassing 'Net'
but we're not at full capacity just yet.

Like the oil in the ground, there's still more to be found,
as the melting ice gives us access to the sea
that gives us much more possibility.

We pay our managers very well; I mean the ones who control their countries
and whose souls they sell.
Oil, yes, they understand how it is to rule a land; they've been paid to tell a tale,
so now we've added fracking for some shale.

We're allowed again to penetrate the land under the sea,
for a little oil just for you and me.

Ok, so we know it's getting hot,
but we have no choice in the matter for all you have must be bought,
and that money that you do pay, goes to us every day.
We get richer at such a speed, it's as if we really have a need,
truth be told, we have more than we can spend,
but the system's made and it´s fixed,
there's no way we'll change our tricks.

We'll distract you all the way, complain and we'll reduce your pay,
and if you're in a land where your rights are even less,
we'll just cause a revolution and distract you with a bloody mess.
You are billions allowed to breed for the slaughter,
and once you're dead we still have your son or daughter,
and when you're dead and gone they will carry on.
The superfluous of the population we can lose in so many ways,
we'll make you ill with what we do,
and then we'll sell you drugs to sooth you some days,
you will think you're happy for a while,
we've given you cheap phones with a smile,

now you've joined our 'consumer plot',
for all you have, it must be bought.

Trapped into our web of lies and deceit,
you can trust us, we'll tell you it's a treat,
as time passes and the show goes on,
well, you'll die a poorly death and then you will be gone,
but before then we will let you breed,
so that you will have more children that will grow up for our need.'

The 'consumer plot', once you're born, you're bought.

A Word from the Poor

We'd like to say we understand why the rich destroy every land,
and yes of course we'd like to have some money too.
You having lots of money is not the problem,
it's how you got it and what you the rich did and do.

You show no compassion for your fellow beings.
You steal the bread and homes of the already poor and desperate.
You make us wear the crown of austerity upon our already heavy head.
You make us wish on many a day that we're dead.

You cannot empathize with the poor in your own land
and for those in war-torn areas of our planet,
you really do not understand;
how some struggle every day
for some food and water they cannot pay.

You demand a lot from us for your wealth,
you demand we die after living a life that was a lie.
You told us we have democracy, no-one believes this anymore
and when your paid-for politicians repeat those words every night
as in a play, there are none that believe those hollow words they say.
We have no leaders that can lead; this we know for sure,
for they are like you now - rich -
bought and bred to lead the world of the dead.

And yes, we are the dead and the dying, it's no exaggeration to say,
many of us die every minute of every day.
It's such a shame you let the world go this horrendous way.
We the poor, you do not really see.
You cannot empathize or care with how it is to be
trodden upon. You have no compassion for us, the poor;
to you we are simply the manure - of the human race.
You let us breed for your need to have slaves to make your toys.
Sometimes we get loud and make some noise,
you play with us like a carrot and a stick,
if we don't bite; you beat us with it with all your might,
or use another trick.

And you are mighty this is true, rich and powerful, it's nothing new.
No, what would be new would be change, a change of thought,
to realize the pain you cause and yes it is you the rich,
you make these laws.

Leaders of compassion, leaders who care,
they are lacking everywhere,
we have a planet full of ordinary people who care,
who don't want to go to war and die,
who don't want their children bombed from the sky,
for what, for oil? To make some people rich,
you kill millions of us to scratch your financial itch.

Most people have a conscience, most people care,
most people would love a world of peace,
and we all know we have enough food to feed all
so that famines would cease.
Everyone could have a life of plenty;
instead we have billions of plates that are empty.

So dear rich and powerful it's not about the money that you have,
it's about what you did and what you now do,
it's about our planet that's slowly burning and it will burn you too.
Nothing saves us from a planet that heats,
in the blowbacks that will come there will be no treats.
Above a certain temperature - everything dies.

You've Been Occupied

It would be wonderful if the so called 'Guardians' and 'leaders' of our world had a
highly developed sense of 'Being',
to be humanly concerned about other sentient beings,
human or otherwise.
Our leaders lack 'Being': for they were not educated 'to be'.

Seekers of power will as an occupational hazard, lack a personal development of
being. Seekers of truth in general will not seek positions of power.
That unfortunately leaves the door wide open leading to the present situation,
a world of 'being-less' leaders.

We unfortunately have the wrong people 'un'-being the 'guardians'
of the human race.
Difficult to change as it's only them that have a face,
blasted into the public mind.
'We're the ones who will lead you, you are blind.

We are the one eyed man; we are the king of all we find,
this we drive into your mind.
You may be blind but you will see
that we control everything you want to be.
There is no way for you to control
anything that you regard as 'Humanly whole'.

We have unfathomable powers of expression; we can see in your
mind and place any impression.
We make you doubt anything you've found out.
We'll distract you from what you do, with war, with hunger,
with your ability to clearly see,
there's no way we'll let you be,
we'll 'occupy' you with a life of inane triviality.

Oh by the way, we have a brand new phone,
just so you never feel alone,
we'll make a deal, in a while we'll make it cheap,
once we've taken all we can reap.
You'll be connected so much so, that we'll know wherever you go,
so you see it's not possible for you anymore to be alone,

even when you close your door, there's nothing that you can say or do,
that we don't know about it too.
Ain't that cool and ain't that neat, there's no way you can us unseat from our
position of power, enjoy the shower, it's gonna rain,
you won't feel it, we'll sell you drugs that kill the pain,
we have interests in this domain.'

How to kill a Hero

'Occupy the poor, treat them like manure, let them breed we have a need, a multiple of bodies to do the dirty work of cleaning the streets, going off to our wars and buying our treats. Of bodies we have a large need. They'll be so busy with all their struggles to survive, there's no way they will change their place in our hive. And yes, they are the workers, this is true, with surveillance everywhere, we can see exactly what you do.

There's another analogy that works as well; we have a large web of deceit, and you the poor are threaded; the invisible web of modern control, it's constantly telling us our hive is whole, if there's a tingle going through the sky, we pick it up going bye, and we know just what to do, your life, has now become see-through.

So be a Hero if you dare, in a moment we'll be there; we have bodies we pay to us protect, we pay them well, they don't suspect, that they are simply one of you. It's a cool trick from times past, we pay some of you to look after you, it's all enabled in the social mass - education we supply, we keep it minimum so you don't understand that you live the lie; sure you will protest now and then, but that just gives us more powers of control, we manipulate it so.

How to kill a Hero? Occupy him; keep him asleep in his dreams; social drugs, media shows, sports, anything it seems. People seem to think it's a metaphor, when in reality, it's literally true, that's cool for us too. Welcome to the game of life, this is the stage of horror of your human play, King Cap rules every day; you may be many and we may be few, but we know the rules and know what to do.'

Cat-food...mmm...tastes good

Some old lady who lived her long life,
who could only afford cat-food at the end of all her strife,
what a fate to meet; some societies are a dead end street.
Cat-food stains on her clothes, with the cat missing, dead she knows.
Her time will be over soon, her last companion gone and dead,
now, she only has memories in her head,
images of her past, but there she sits before a plate,
eating cat-food is her fate.

The sadness of a life to meet that end,
so many old now on cat-food do depend,
who's to blame, the old or the government who rule in our name?
They rule over us, that's for sure, but they treat us like manure.

****

"Allow the poor to breed, for a mass of bodies we have a need,
when they get old and can no longer serve,
well, they have cat-food in reserve
that will do them till they die, they're the poor, they know why.

Consider yourself lucky if you have a home, and we don't chuck you in the street,
and day and night you must roam, sleeping in doorways or in a cardboard box,
or under a bridge or under rocks.
We don't care, we have your money now and you're old,
you knew it was coming, you were told,
struggle or die; it's your fate coming bye.

Be happy with your God, ours is rich, he looks after us well,
you he shod and sent to hell. Enjoy your life in the street,
and if you still have a home, well, enjoy the cat-food it's a treat.

Of course we do pretend to care,
we're educated, we have many words we can spare,
but reality bites at the end.

We say we sympathise, but we just pretend,
we're actors in a play, we say it different every day.
The cool part is that you believe
some of the words we use to you deceive.
Cat-food…mmm…tastes good."

****

The young people of the world today,
look at them - before you look away.
No matter how they be now – they are our future – somehow.
They will become the Heroes that all the world needs,
and if we fail the young today, then we condemn them to not only eat Cat-food
when their old, if that they can find, for we've turned our world
into the planet of the blind.

****

It's predicted that civilization will collapse and fall.
When there's not enough food to eat,
barbarism will roam our streets.
And after all the other animals die out,
the only other flesh to be found,
well, it will be the other poor still around.

With pen in hand, signature in ink,

Laws were made, humanity began to sink.

King Capitalist the Cruel

When he reigned, it rained upon us all.

We have been led into a world of horror,
where the Hot sun will dry our children and theirs to the bone;
by men who only sought profit to make,
and they only looked after their own.

A world of dying desperation - the needy dropped like flies.
Austerity rages for countless years without cessation.
The poor were dropping all around;
there was no food to be found.

The children's pain cut like a knife,
it was short, but that was their life.
It wasn't much – a life of pain.
There was so much more to gain.

****

Now, you can call it Doom and Gloom if you will.
Granted you may just want to get on with life, and not think about all
this stuff that will be in the future human strife.
But as most people who don't have their heads buried in the sand
seem to slowly understand: the causes for our woes today.

Just in case you're very rich and don't know the troubles that you stitch,
let's remind you of a few, measures inflicted on almost all,
as the poor pay for the rich to have a ball.

****

Methods of attraction and distraction occupy our energy and time.
Tired from overwork or media induced banalities,
none left for social, common and human change,
all that's kept above us, just out of range.

Manipulated and embedded by methods of suggestion
'You'll like what we sell, it's not a question.
Organised and educated to hate others not of your colour,
keeps you separate and apart,
it directs your energy and anger to them, it's a cool art.

Racial equality - it has never really been so,
but for a while we had to let you think it was happening down below.
Sure, we let some coloureds rise up to the top
but only if it suits us, if it doesn't, that we stop,
because mostly for now, brown or black suffer our merciless attack.

In our prisons we make you work, almost for free -
hell - this is better than when we called it slavery,
and we don't find that anything is wrong;
denial is our Egyptian river song.

Enjoy your protests in the street our police have been militarized,
ain't that sweet? No more keepers of the peace, but our law
and our order – that won't cease.

When we capture you, down you will go,
if it's not from bullets and you survive
well you'll become another in our prison work hive –
and then we'll occupy you for almost all your life,
you will never see your child or your wife.

And when this is done to enough of you, well, down the social ladder you will drop,
social security is just a stop,
until you'll all be in the streets
and because we'll make that illegal too
it will be off to prison, there's still work to do.

You're our slave labour in our camps;
we'll punish you if you don't lick our boots and stamps.
It's took a while for you to see that this is how we planned it to be.

****

Social and racial inequality it's such a cool tool
for 'King Capitalist the Cruel'.
Of course that's only one aspect of our distraction,

there are many that we use; after all we have a world to abuse.
And it's ready and waiting for the taking too,
we'll eat it all and leave none for you.

Oh by the way, how's the War?
Where you don't know what you're fighting for.
We told you just the other day, did you forget?
A little freedom and a democratic say.

Remember, remember; we allowed you the common people to have a vote,
well, we had no choice
you were nearly storming the castle and crossing the moat.
So we let you think you had a voice
but truth be told - we left you no choice.
We think it's really fun; we have slaves with nowhere to run.
There is nowhere else to go; you're in the social structure show.

All the world's a stage
and we have many of you to fill the roles we gave,
we let you breed we had a need,
but now you're plenty we make you bleed.
In older times we hung you from a tree,
well, now we don't have to, we embedded how this should be,
be happy with your app, you're traced on all our maps.'

Part two

At home he was a really sweet guy. He had kids, they'd watch T.V. he'd hug them when they'd cry. They'd watch wildlife and say 'dad isn't that sad?' He'd say 'yes son, that's bad.' He had many ways to show that sympathy he did know. But he was a little bit like Jekyll and Hyde, for in the morning on the way to work, King Cap the Cruel would ride.

He'd dawn his robes for the day, a suit and tie with something to say. He was a King in his own way. Those who knew him called him 'King Cap the Cruel' for short. Life for him was anything that could be bought, he had a 'Midas touch' in a way, for if he was annoyed, everything he touched, he destroyed.

To make profit was the aim of the game and he played it very well, he was King Cap the Cruel, his bank account did swell. The policies he implemented affected people through the world, within days of his signature with pen in ink, many lives began to sink. People-Peasants thrown out of land and home, lived on the streets only to roam. Ah, King Cap the Cruel, he ruled from afar, he never saw the misery he unleashed from the jar: from the jar of tricks, a box, one from Pandora's stocks.

King Cap signs a deal and thousands of people disappear, fallen down the social structure, their life goes towards its fate, eating Cat-food at their end, before their departure date. King Cap the Cruel, he's nobody's friend. Sometimes he's aware of this and sometimes he's not, but his conscience he sold and a big yacht he bought. But not only; he bought his fate, for him now a different path awaits.

****

Something solidifies deep within, in older times they called it an unholy sin or missing the mark. When what you do causes so much pain and suffering the world through and is only dark, then your fate is fixed and it's been sealed, the Game of Death you have revealed.

King Cap the Cruel, this he does not think, from his own truth he does drink, his psychology has been amended, for this job he was recommended by others who drink and eat from the same table of despair, destruction, and death; it's called the table of D's and the only word they like is please. But; it's a word you never hear them say, no compassion nor empathy gets through in any way. King Cap the Cruel rules the day.

Bright Morning

Part one

24-7-365 – everyday, Hell on Earth, but still alive.

The Sun warming up the day,
as she lay there she felt the warmth of the sun's ray.
Upon her face the atoms danced,
her toes, they twinkled,
for atoms, it was romance.
She stretched and yawned and knew she must rise,
for she always rose at the coming dawn.
She slept so well that night
she didn't want to move and enter the day and fight.

But fight she must to survive,
for the doorway in which she slept would soon come alive.
She had a night of peaceful rest,
but usually nights were an awesome test,
to make it through without an attack,
where she must find a place to sleep
with a wall behind her back.

Most nights now she could never sleep safe and sound
there were always dangers, all around.
Her body was not aged, nor grotesque;
there were always men that would contest
to be first, to take what was not theirs, to have or hold.

When she was younger she was loved – she was told,
and she felt love when she was young.
But she got into a little debt
and the government treated her like an unwanted pet.
Thrown out into the street,
the life of poverty she did meet.

With her family all dead or gone,
there was nowhere she did belong.
Too ashamed to seek out friends of old,

for she's a loser, society told.
When you can't pay your way
you lose your home and your say.
Nowhere to live, nowhere to go,
Carry your valuables down below.
With no food to eat,
life becomes a dead end street.

****

People look happy as they play with their phones,
so busy with somewhere to go and something to do.
You have a home, I'm happy for you.

****

Time to move, the day begins,
she must find food before they empty all the bins.
The search for scraps to eat – anything is always a treat,
otherwise an empty day to beg with an empty hand,
and hope some people with pity will understand;
that this is not how she wants to live,
for it's not a life – she knows that deep,
every night she does weep.
There is never a moment of caring love;
there is no grace from above.

She must always find a new place to sleep,
if you're attacked in one place
from behind you don't see their face,
they will hold you down and take their turn
as your inside begins to burn.

High on a girder, upon a bridge can be safe and good
if you're so high you're not their food,
but you have to tie yourself in to sleep
and when the wind blows you always weep.
How long can she live this way?
She takes it day by day.

The government said 'We care about you,
but for now you'll have to make your own way;
we know you will you do all and anything to survive,
after all, it's natural, everybody fights to stay alive.

But as to how you live and what you must do,
we'll leave that up to you,
when you have new work and earn a little pay,
remember, you still owe us money, pay it back one day.

We have a motto, we have a creed,
'all you have, we really need.'
We must pay for the wars you fight;
we don't care how you survive the night.
We have bosses that we must please;
we lick their jackboots as we're on our knees.
And eventually everybody's on their knees.

I know you have no money and no bed,
but you look sweet, how's your head?'

****

The government official parted from the sweet girl,
and as he left he said, 'Here's some money before we part;
yes, I know I have a heart.
Here's an euro, or a pound, or a dollar, today they're sound,
it will help you buy a loaf of bread,
and if you're lucky they will offer free cake to taste,
remember, don't let that go to waste.'

****

Yes, the government has a heart,
it's yours; they take it when you from your house they part.
They close the house and board it up.
Wait awhile until they can sell,
it's a capitalists' democracy, you can tell.

'So dear poor, young, or old,
if you have no bread or cake to eat,
try some cat-food we hear it's a treat.

And if you can't even that afford,
well, kill a cat, we have too many on board.
We're sure they roast up very well,
and it keeps the streets clean of their smell.

It's one of our Austerity measures,
supplying lots of cats for your pleasures.
All these fires we see burning in the night,
at first we thought it was protests until we realized the sight,
little cats on a stick, hell – Austerity is a really cool trick.
With a little salt and pepper on the side,
a cat may taste like chicken,
but don't eat too many, there you might sicken.

And if you get crazy in the street, don't worry, we don't.
We have places just for you, the public pay, sad, but true.

Don't worry about what in there we do;
we've got experts trained to look after you,
and they carry a stick or an electric shock
when they're finished you can't talk,
but then you never had anything to say before,
except 'I'm sorry' when we knocked on your door.

We took your house and your life;
we turned you out into the street, to live this strife,
to lock you up in the end.
So we can tell the poor public we do this for you,
we lock these violent, dangerous, homeless, unwanted and
nameless individuals up for your safety, it's our concern.
You pay a little on your tax, on your return.

This is how our system of Austerity works,
you voted us into power, so who's to blame,
we simply hold the cards and deal, it's all a game,
the game of life, of course there is much more to see,
this is just one method of our Austerity.'

****

The river of her life began one day to decline.
The currents of life's events became too strong,
she was lost and she was not where she did belong.
She often slept on a girder high on a bridge, and late at night from above;
it was like the voices of angels going by.
She never saw their face, just heard the joy of the human race.

Before life became so bad she was concerned about Global Warming,
she thought that awfully sad.
What a way for humans to go, spiralling down like a helter skelter show.
What a fate for our kids to meet,
we leave our children a warming treat.
Sometimes in her days now those old thoughts flashed through her mind,
but it was like another life - now - she was blind.

When you eat no nourishing food, anything is good,
but it never feeds your mind when you have to eat anything you find.
She wondered why the really rich let all this stuff happen,
they lost their soul in their journey through life.
Perhaps they were chucked out of their soul, just like she was from her
house and home - Left alone to roam.

Bright Morning

Part Two
she made it through the summer

24-7-365 – everyday, Hell on Earth, but still alive.

She crumpled up warm and cosy,
wrapped up like a Christmas present,
enjoying the trapped heat that kept her warm, feeling good and alive.

Her belly still full from the 'cordon blue' burger
she found discarded in the street,
by some drunken youths passing bye, too drunk to eat.
To her 'z38' was a wonderful treat.
A chemical in food, whose only function was to stop you from being sick;
from mass produced food companies, it was a really neat trick.

Time to wake and move for the day,
the old warm newspapers she put away.
They kept her warm that night through,
stuck inside her clothing, her hand-made duvet;
it was the best she knew.

One night, not too long ago,
some men took her body and then her sleeping bag too,
left her in the dark of night,
full of pain still, her eyes were open in the coming beautiful morning light,
but from then till now, newspapers she did read.

Libraries, ahh, wonderful places of warmth to sit and read,
sadly, they were closing all around,
the government made them bleed.
To be allowed inside those doors, if they were to be found,
you had to be clean or at least not to smell.
The poor were never to be seen.

The unwanted and untouchables of our society,
they must be left to die.

If only they would hurry up is the thought, if not the cry.
Empathy or sympathy for the poor and destitute, mmm... just a little but mostly,
the so called 'good people' are mute.

****

The government continue in their ways,
'We have wars to finance and you must pay,
so we'll cut through you with Austerity, it's our knife,
we don't care if you suffer or take your own life.
We let you breed, of bodies we have a need,
it's true, now we have so many;
it seems as if we don't know what to do,
but we have many ways where we can get rid of thousands of you.
We'll keep the young unemployed and send them off to war and kill,
we embed it so they think it's a thrill, they will meet with realities of horror and hell,
if they come back, they won't be well.

We fixed the laws so prison has a high demand,
the tax for that we take from you, we hope you understand,
it's hidden within a monster-mix law, sorry, we thought you knew.
Well now you do, but we don't care,
we've manipulated your thought, watch T.V. and just stare,
have fun with your reality T.V. show,
poor or punished is the only one you'll know.'

****

Her mind wandered just like her body through the streets,
sometimes nice thoughts visited, those were treats
or memories of times past,
romantic moments, but they didn't last.
So many thoughts and images passed through her head,
but she knew she wouldn't make it much longer,
soon she'd be dead.

As she gathered up her things, she knew her body weakened.
Life here on Earth was rough; she packed her stuff
in a plastic bag that was life now, a bag lady of the street.
Her husband died; they took away her children
and left her all alone, survive or die was the cry.
If you want to see your children ever again,

come back when money is your friend.

Well, it's winter now and life fares no better than before,
she will die before she ever enters another home sweet home door.
Truth be told, she was bold.
Her power to survive was strong,
but luck was against her, in a society that was all wrong.
These things she did not think,
from another cup she did drink.

Her mind was clear,
but there was nothing to hold onto that was near,
for sadness ripped her heart apart,
if only from the beginning she could again start.
Not for her-self, for that she did not care,
but for her children that must grow up without her being there.

She fell dramatically down the social structure of this crown.
She had studied in the past,
before she had her kids, but as they got into debt,
the good times didn't last.
She just moved into a new town,
no friends to help, no-one around.
No family couch to crash or sleep in safety,
her heart and spirit broke, when the government stole her kids.
They forced her into the street for her fate to meet,
and meet it she did.

She made it through the summer, 24-7-365,
every day, hell on earth, but still alive.

****

Winter's here now, but she won't make it through,
there's no-one to talk to, nothing to do.
She was ashamed to be seen, when she begged for a coin,
it was as if her old life had never been.

With her last energy before she died,
she curled her body and in a photo cried.
Her kids who were somewhere but nowhere to be found,
the photo lay in her hand and her hand upon the ground,

her body frozen, cold as ice.
She died a lonely death one cold winter night in the street,
this women who had her fate to meet.

'Captain my captain', you lead us to Hell

Captain my captain, your soul you did sell.

When the captain of a ship has gone mad
and is leading the crew over the edge and in many ways bad,
mutiny has often been the cry;
it starts from lower down and travels up high.

The poor people live in fear; the rich desire it, that's clear.
It helps to keep the poor this way,
all over the world, separate, no say.
It serves the rich very well;
the poor must do what the rich do tell.

'Dominate and separate, women and equal rights,
blacks from whites,
middle class from below and above.
To fear minorities in every land,
be a bigot, a racist or a dominating male,
so that if you try to unite, you will always fail.

All we do is press a switch, we've got lots we're the rich.

Lots of employees in our system, it's you the confused herd,
the cattle we raise and slaughter,
when you're dead we'll use your son or your daughter.
It's only one system we use today,
of course sometime it will wash away,
something better might come that has even more control,
another system, this is a pre-show.

It might become a religious police state,
that way we control everything, even your fate,
for we will write it in our creed, you must die for our need,
then you will be happy to serve till the day you die,
until we send you up to your heaven in the sky.
Religious control that's a cool treat;

we tried democracy but this you now see through
things take time, but meanwhile we had a ball, we'll add in a few more twists and
turns, we'll twist the knife until it burns.
Killed a few million all over the world;
left violence, poverty and death everywhere.

We have a world wide web of deceit,
so there's no way we will change this treat.
You can try to make us if you will,
but if you survive, you'll pay a large hospital bill,
and to pay for that you will go deeper into debt.
You're nothing but our human pet. We don't need to lock you in chains anymore,
you have media and technology, that's our door, our entry into your house and
home, nowhere you go will you ever be alone, we can track your every move,
and our technology will improve.'
Love
your owner. The Captain x

Who Won?

It seems there are many that call for revolution,
in all corners of the world.
Of course this is a path to much death and destitution.
When governments are corporate-owned
and public rights have been 'boned' - down to the core,
that may leave people with no option but the revolution door.

Then of course eventually it shall come to pass,
that the people will revolt 'en masse'.
The rich with their private laws have been unbelievably crass.
To care is only a 'thing' that a better understanding could bring,
and if politicians have been bought,
then 'to care' is something that they never thought.

"Let them eat cake", was said by Marie Antoinette before she lost her head,
when she was told the poor had no bread.
So out of touch with reality, she was of the rich that did not see
that not only did the poor have no bread.
They had no cake that she was stuffing into her head.

****

Today the situation is the 'same but different' from that war of class,
the powerful have surveillance that can see all the 'mass'.
Combined with 'behavioural engineering', one of the greatest powers of control,
they can deflect the situation with misguided information,
and lead the rabbit further down the hole,
so that people think that all is right - in this darkness of human night.

That gives them the power to divert attention to things of consumer choice,
as paradoxical as it seems,
give them a new phone, they'll have no voice.

The power of the common man is completely taken, about their freedoms,
they were greatly mistaken - through - media mental manipulation, attention,
energy, and free choice have been taken.

*A wall: like many other reminding walls of sadness, destruction and decay – of life
– inner and outer – captured moments, ´Frozen in living time´ passed away.*

With laws in place ready to abuse,
and militarized police with deadly weapons that they already use,
then it's death that will come to many.

Now in this 'state of things' it's getting late,
we basically sealed our planets fate,
societies choice of consume more and more
has led us to an 'un-trodden shore'.
The call is simple 'more' or 'less'
but all humans face this problem.

The poor, those who have less,
or nothing at all:
have different problems most of all,
in Third World Countries, poverty, starvation,
and violent death from everywhere.

****

The population are devastated in the main,
their rights are attacked with no refrain,
'The gloves are off' no letting up,
and that's what leads to calls for revolution,
because the powerful only know one solution.

Strike the poor with a 'mailed fist' of control,
break their body and their soul.
It's as if the rich had no children to awaken,
that feeling inside that cannot be mistaken,
love, compassion and care,
sadly it took a walk and went back down the stair,
of human evolution.

'All for me and none for you', you're dead no matter what you do.
So what shall it be for you and me?
Mmm, is equality just a fantasy?
Some humans seem to lack some connections in their neuron tracks.
Do you think it may be possible to recover from this deadly attack,
to bring a reformation
to help ourselves and all life, recover from this devastation?
'Who won?'   No-one!

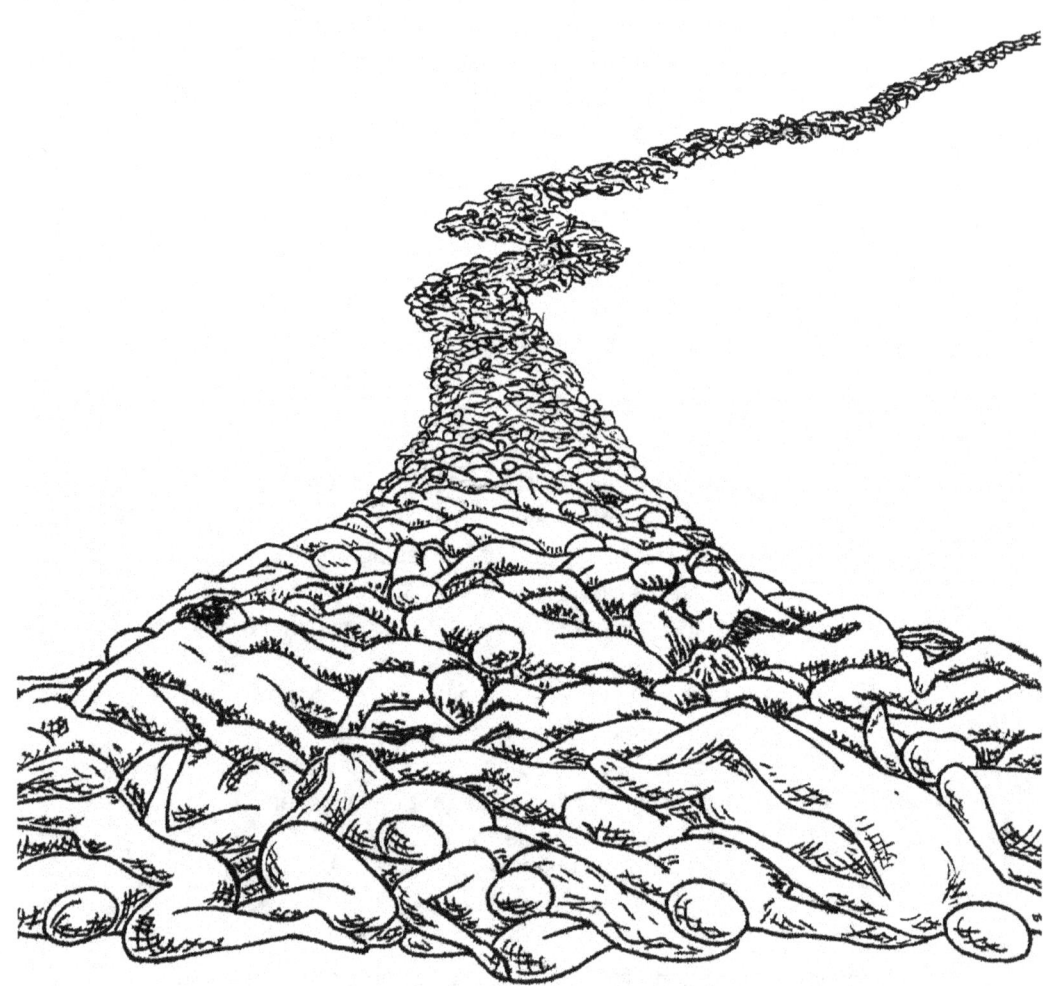

Invaded

mobbing from the rich

When you think there's nothing you can do,
then nothing is what you'll do,
when you think that there may be a way,
where you the 'common man' can speak
then one day perhaps you may.

Hope with fear entwined is a weakness that will bind.
Hope that strengthens you to be bold
will lead to tales to be told
about the strength that lies within all men and women.

Justice only comes from those who are able
to bring another's opinion to the table,
to step into their shoes and see how it is that they be,
otherwise it's just a sham and all they say is just a scam.

****

'Common sense' in a civil society is a counterweight
against a 'crazed state'.
In a democracy, powerful are the seeds of tyranny.
What country can boast of a constitution
that leaves its young and old and poor in destitution?
Powers that be, that rape the population,
by invading their personal life, enter their emails and private phones,
a government that doesn't leave their population alone;
It's a form of mobbing and control,
from a power that has 'Being-less' leaders with no soul.

The oppressors are those who have always been
the rich, the powerful, and the unseen.
Their power lies in the dark, but not only on the side,
they have open projects all around, they don't really have to hide.

The corporation's that were found,
are sending humankind downward bound,
there has been a 'war on reason',

for ever since the word was thought,
it was sold and slaves were bought.
But not only in bondage are we held,
manipulated consumerism is a power that they weld,
free speech is now no more,
if it ever was,
people live in fear from someone knocking on their door.

****

The revolt against repression in many lands
was a result of people suffering pain.
Global managers handled it well,
it was contained.
A burning fire of burning flesh
of some poor boy who wanted out the mesh,
which traps us all in a web of deceit,
no free speech for the common man in the street!

****

'You may struggle and you may strive,
but you're stuck within our hive,
we breed you, we feed you, a little,
so you do hope, but you hope with fear,
for we whisper in your ear,
and that's the weakness we hold dear.

We like it when you fear,
we don't operate on love,
there's nothing higher from above
than us, we have a creed,
'It's all for us and none for you',
and we've got lots of you.

We don't care about your colour, your sex or your age,
or if you complain or even rage,
we have psychologists on our side,
they teach us that we don't have to hide,
we confuse you so you do not really understand,
that all your public institutions are promoting our corporate brands.

You wear our T-shirts that have our names,
made by other kids just for yours,
but we find in that no shame,
for to us you are the breed,
and we have many with your name.

You may be all different colours, in different lands,
but your psychology we understand,
so you will die – but before – you will buy –
that will increase our social standing,
and if you get too demanding,
we'll blow you up from the sky.

****

If you live within our cities and closer to our supporting structure,
if you 'cheat' us with a little rupture,
well, that's really no big deal,
we can read about what you do and how you really feel,
it's just as if we can read your mind.
You're our mice and you are blind,
we have conditioned you to pretend
that there's a little hope around the bend,
there's a leaver, for a reward, you can pull,
but you'll always be our fool.

****

We keep you occupied with fashion and survival,
we give you film and T.V. and my oh my, that has no rival.
We keep you stuck in your imagination,
the door was opened, there's no cessation.

This is life and how it is to be,
for at least another hundred years or more,
because Global Warming's at our door.
To keep you breeding in our hive and to maintain you alive,
we need energy to sustain the factory of pain,
we've burned a planet, all in your name.'
Humankind, the wise-man indeed.

'Bridge Makers'

Healing of the Nations

You are the bridge makers one and all,
regardless to the name of your call.
Between one world and another,
between a man's lower and his higher,
to bridge them, we can but aspire,
to build a bridge is a healing of the nations.
To find a common cause and a common relation –
to bring the balance back – to build this bridge in the here and now,
to return again and again – now.

If the bridge-makers live up to their name,
they will find things much the same, but different,
but they need this moment now to reclaim.

Sense yourself; your time is near
where you may suddenly make a bridge appear.
To build a bridge that you must first cross
in order that others do not get lost.
Lost, of course we all are, to find ourselves we travel far,
but the only journey worth really making
is the one we've been forsaking,
into the labyrinth of the self, you, in this moment now,
sense your breath, begin somehow.

There will be moments where you can see – yourself
standing on top, of the bridge called I - me.
Your body is the foundation from one end till the other.
Fathers and Mothers of Being – become aware of yourself as you're seeing;
hold the moment, as you would hold a bow
– you are the arrow – let it go –

Don't think about what it should be. Can you perceive it silently?
Hold the moment, you are the bridge,
suspend this moment of time - now.
With humility become aware, no conceit must be there.
The bridge has steps and they're never straight,

you know it's no easy path to Heaven's gate.
But none the less there's a ladder, there's a stair,
there's a bridge which is a path, it's called 'Being there'.

Only you can bring a balance back - to yourself.

To bring a balancing of the tensions, to equalize the sensing,
then you may hold that moment more,
it's like drawing the arrow to take aim;
if you miss the mark, it's not a shame,
for you can hold the moment and become aware, anytime,
if you dare, it becomes a choice of what do you serve.

From books of rules we must break, to follow a path we must take –
time is now counted - there are no long term plans in the making,
humanity now we are forsaking.
Our planet heats quicker than it should,
the bridge-makers must draw humanity together and none exclude.

'The unreal has no Being, the real never ceases to be' -
'even if you have broken your vow a thousand times, come, come again'.
Draw the arrow a thousand times more to bring that balance back,
you've been asleep a'while, welcome back.

STEAL

Secret trade Economic Austerity Laws

To make secret laws and control the trade,
and in the dark they sharpen their claws for the people to be slayed.
To allow companies to control what they sought,
then our politicians who agree have been bought.
When it's the people who in the end will lose
as paid for politicians did the public abuse.

The rich have fixed it in the laws of all lands,
that the poor shall stay uneducated about these criminal bands
and that there is little to be done under a warming sun.

Trading your rights for a good common cause:
suggestions sent down from above, could it be love?
Humans tied to an incredible wheel
as it gets spun around our rights and monies they steal.
The common people in every land,
this is something they now understand,
so there are struggles and protests everywhere now;
people protest just to survive
to have common rights just to stay alive.

The rich and powerful will not give way;
struggles are only won day by day.
The people need to have one cause,
it will need new Global Warming Laws.

So far so un-good, the agreements are a con,
it will never achieve what we need
and nothing will change while we are dispersed like seeds,
but that may well be a seed of change
for with a Global Warming no-one's out of range.

It doesn't take much to make the world right,
get rid of those that profit, put them out in this dark night.
They've locked the path of human progress
and left our planet in a mess.
Most human troubles you can relate
back to those who make policy control and have the keys of the gate.

They've trashed our planet. Keepers of culture they are not,
they finance Art, but only stuff that can be bought,
they don't finance the human way - about human rights
and Global Warming they have nothing to say.

It only takes a few billions to feed the worlds' poor,
but it takes trillions to kill them and bury them for manure.
Human slaves born and bred
mostly left unfed. And we need leaders for that!
Calling them slave traders would be closer to the mark.

Being-less leaders are not leaders.
Fixed in the system, systematic that way,
where controllers of might have the last say.
Well, these are laws that are not real,
that's why they're called STEAL.

Revolution or Reform
A planet 'too big to fail'

Revolution or reform
everything's on sale

Some call for revolution, but that would bring a storm;
it would leave many in destitution,
when what we need is a world of reform.

Reforming policies that were made
and that the poor have always paid.

Revolutions bring violence in their wake, is it possible to have a peaceful revolution
of solid constitution, where people come to themselves with a voice and a cause,
one that resonates above all the trivia and the unjust laws.

The world of course has been under an attack of under-consideration of social inequality and over-consumption of all that we see.
We thought we could feed off the world and it could still be.

But nothing's for nothing and nothing ever remains the same,
is it man or capitalism to take the blame?

****

A 'Man-Being' what he is, will always attract a life of strife,
this we all recognize in some way,
but regardless, there is an aim to be made by the young of today,
there's a time limit to adhere to what must be done,
of course it's pretty heavy to think that the future depends on you,
but perhaps there's something, however small, you can do.
Only you will know, if you can,
help the future of this being called man.

The older generation unfortunately are old,
that sense of everything achievable has gone cold,
in general this is always so,
but you the young have that wonderful possibility and enthusiasm always to know.
It's an energy that comes with youth,
it's wisdom before it has been ripened with experience
and often disappointments of high expectations.

Are these expectations too high? To request of yourself not to live the lie,
but to see the reality that is all around, something's been lost
only in the youth of the world can it be found?
Older experience can guide a way,
but it's you the youth who have that power today.

****

A Revolution or Reform, we have a planet too big to fail,
a revolution of thought can be brought, by the youth of today,
a reform of personal – social – country – world policies,
only the youth can truly influence the say.
It can become a wonder and a delight, but it needs a spark
that becomes a flame, that burns in your name. Can you be that spark?
Can you be that flame? For it needs many candles
all over the world, individual, but much the same.

It's difficult, you know it is - a soft revolution of thought and care
but you can always remember earth somewhere.
The older generation has always known that when they're violent it will return;
only destruction does that wheel turn.
It's been used and manipulated all through time,
and it's always the young, the poor, the weak who pay a heavy fine.
The war on 'anything' is always rebranded to 'their' cause,
those who are rich and in charge, and create oppressive laws.

To cut a long story in half
15 years and the fire's at the gate,
you dear youth do not have time to wait,
you're being occupied by anything and all;
you're being blinded just before the fall.
Occupied by consciously maintained trivia,
you know the list, it's almost endless,
you know yourself there's much that's senseless,

but what do you think, what do you feel? Is this so called reality real?
When there's a fire outside the door
the house will burn while we're being told to only want more.

More of what we got, which off course must be bought,
you're not being asked to give up all,
simply start a revolution of thought, where care must become the call
those means and methods of control,
all of those of which you know,
you see it, you hear it, you feel it every day.
Reform the world - because you really do have a say.

15 years to bring a change,
it's on a speeding train heading out of range,
it's lonely in space way out there,
raise your voice, start a soft movement of planetary care.

We're the Rich -
Revolution or Reform?

**We are where we belong,
we sing our song
'yes we can'
and you too will sing along**

Revolution or reform, take your pick,
we're the rich; they're both a trick,
so do whatever you can do, we'll control it through and through,
look at all the things we have done and can do.
We control the government and say when to go to war;
we control the media and tell you what you're fighting for.

We influence the policy of all that affects you,
we know exactly what to do, it's been a while in the making,
but a world so rich in resources is well worth our taking.

Of course we pay a lot for this evil pleasure,
but we worked out how to make it tax deductible, it's in our measure.

So in reality you do pay for how we treat you every day,
we even work it that the police protect us and do what we say.

And if you protest at all, they'll come knocking on your door at night,
steal your wife, your kids, your life
and you'll have no power or will to fight.

We leave you in a world where you must struggle to survive
often where you're lucky, just to be alive.

If your skin is one of colour and you live in other lands,
believe me, we'll force you to understand,
if you have anything that we want or need,
we will take it, for we have a creed,
'all for me and none for you',
there really is nothing you can do.

We can start a revolution and keep it under our control,
many of you will not survive and no family will be whole.
If we discover something in your land,
we - will - take - it - and - you - will - understand
that there's nothing you can do.

We might leave you some, but not too much,
if you don't bow down to what we suggest;
we'll leave a bullet in your chest.
You see, we've got coffers that are never full,
you the common people must pay the bill,
there's so many of you that you should by now understand,
you cannot have any piece of land.

But we have a facade to keep in place,
as we're the elite of the human race,
we are rich and you are not, everything you don't have, we have got.

We donate to charities,
it's nice to have an unspoken competition,
to help the poor who are on their knees,
that way we alleviate suspicion,
of what it is that we really are,
a supporter of the 'Goddess' called PR.

She's a Goddess we adore, we drop our riches at her door,
and her rewards are always in the making, for you the public,
'The silent herd' are forsaking, your life and liberty,
it's no longer yours, but ours for the taking.

She's manipulated your thought,
now, everything that you think, you bought.
It's a rich reward from the goddess of PR.
For the media has manipulated you to stray from who you really are.
You are kept 'occupied' with trivia
- which you must buy - to keep up the appearance
- of the life that lives the lie.

Of course we let you think you have a voice,
but we have a really great trick, we supply the choice,
so in the end you will comply, you will live the lie.
Of that, some of you will of course see.
We call it 'well managed democracy'.
It's a really super tool; we call it 'the poor man's fool'.

If we hear you make a rumble,
we'll pull some strings and you will stumble,
down and trodden, we'll 'occupy' you,
by the time we're finished you won't know what to do.

We keep you trampled and 'a p a r t' we don't let you solidify.

And if anytime you decide to take back the 'commonality' of what is really yours,
well, we can see you coming, we're wired and we're ready, for everything now that
you do, we can see and hear it too.

Plans were made long ago, and we have more in the making,
your public rights are just a show, it was long and painstaking,
but now we are where we want to be,
'none for you and all for me'.

Try the cake if there's any left;
just remember the name of the play
it was called 'Theft'.

All your systems based on solidarity, we destroy them wantonly,
we send progression and society back towards the past,
there is no way your methods will us outlast.
We have powerful and well paid friends controlling at the top,
we're the predator species and we can't really stop;
we will eat all we can, down till the end of man.

As to your 'Global Warming', well yes, there's truth to that,
but we're the predator species and we have you trapped,
and there's nowhere else to go, for us it's no big deal,
the warming sun we don't have to feel, (just yet)
so 'all's well that ends well' for us.

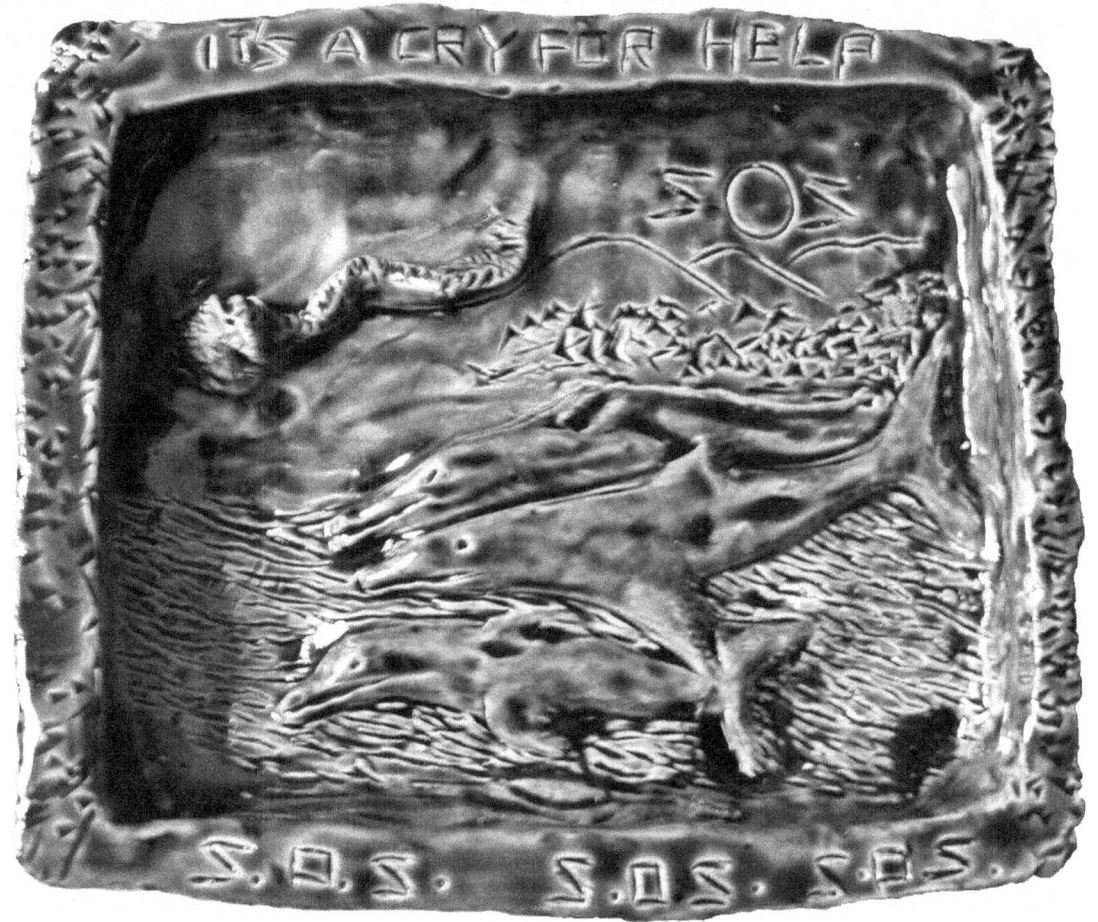

Sadness of Society - SOS

Organized Austerity

The leaders of the world seemed to have no moral center to work from or to return, now our planet will sadly burn. Another hundred years of technological invention: they'll combine people's genes, so they'll control the lie we live and the dream. When the people in charge and control have no moral center, then they will allow all sorts of horrors on our Earth to be. They do not externally pay the price of the sadness of this society; they make their money and are well paid, but humanity they enslaved.

Their secret and not so secret wars with words manipulated to hide the truth of evil acts. It was war from above, a merciless attack, multisided and different over all our world. Laws were made and they dealt with their devil inside; man has the possibility for good and bad, there's always the opposite of happy, it's called sad. A common goodness should have been the guide and the light, to lead humanity on a dark night; and this time now, becomes the darkest night of our soul – humankind: ruled from down below.

Lost all contact to the higher that lies within, the rich and powerful fed their dragon; there is no escaping from this sin. And sin is probably the right word to use, for the concept of goodness they did abuse. They missed the mark and it was clear, humankind will disappear.

There's an evil to behold in the works of the rich and powerful; it's been clearly told, for they advertise it in advance, it's just they use so many words, so it sounds like romance. Their key was distraction and attraction: distract the poor with struggles in their every day: attract them to buy things and be occupied in different ways.

****

"They will struggle in the world we've made; they don't even know they've been enslaved. It's all a pretense, it's all a show; we let them think they are free, but shadows on a wall, is all they see. We confuse them with technological wizardry. We gave them newly developed toys, it stops the neurons in their brain from working and making new connections; to see that there was another world to be. To be or not, makes no difference; they've been bought.

We offered them a world of plenty, but we kept half of them poor and their bellies empty; spread across the lands under different names of corporate brands. We monopolized up a scale, we joined together, we never fail. We are the super-rich, we have a motto, 'ain't life a bitch', all for us and none for you and there's nothing you can do. You struggle in the mess we've made - hell - you don't even realize it yet, you've been enslaved.

Slaved in bondage or in debt, you're our little human pet. We like it like that, you're so sweet, we give you movies; you think it's a treat, but we embed the evil that we plan, you didn't know it but we turn you into the lowest form of man. We have to do it that way, our level of being means we have no other say. And we are the darkest of humanity, simply look at our acts and see our insanity, like attracts like and you we spike.

Enjoy everything that we give to you, it's a drug; we make you pay for that too. Speaking of which, in the future, there will be wonderful drugs that we will sell to you, they block the horrors that we will unleash upon humanity; you will enjoy, but be subdued, it stops revolutions from bring renewed.

For a while we outlawed many things of pleasure and addiction, it brought us wealth and you much friction; but slowly we realized how to balance the stick, and yes, it is a stick, we chemically control you to accept our trick; cheap and free for all it will be, produced in foods in the factory. Our chemists are working very hard but lots of stuff are still barred. All the laws we slowly wear down, for we are the real keepers of the crown. We don't need to call ourselves kings anymore we are the masters of the universe - whom you adore.

We sealed it in your education, embedded thought without cessation, T.V. films, and advertisements and then the internet - that surprise was new. But like always we know exactly what to do. It takes a generation or so, that where you're going you'll never really know. It was a war that you did lose, humanity we did abuse. Fear and pleasure are our tools to control the working class; you have been 'slaved' by our rules, yours sincerely the super-rich, upper class: we are the Masters Of the Mass. Just call us 'MOM' for short, for anything you have, your 'MOM' has brought."

CHESS or CHECKMATE ?

Chess - Controlling How Earth Shall Suffer

We win, you lose, our planet we will abuse. We know all the moves to make, after all, our lives are at stake. We have the most powerful pieces in control – we rule this planet whole. Sure your pawns are spread all over the lands but you have no powerful pieces at your command. We can see every move you make and we will burn you at the stake.

Chess is just maths at the end, and we know everything, we just pretend – our PR Goddess told us to play the game this way. Confuse the enemy, let them think they have a say. But our pieces are moving across the planet every day, we control the rules of the game, sacrifice a little here and there, the end result will be the same. We will win this game.

We work 24-7-365 and yes, we know the planet will burn alive, but it's a game in which we are stuck, it's not a game of chance or luck. We didn't realise at the beginning that this would be the end, but the rules of capitalism have been fixed, it's like superglue, we can't change our tricks. So we just enjoy the riches as we go, after all we want to be around to see the end of the show. It will be spectacularly warm at the end, our scientists have told us – we educate and pay them very well, so about their findings – yes, it's a truth they tell.

But this is not a game of chance. You say it's maths, yes, we know it's not romance, it's about survival - we found out first - you think we have no love, compassion or care, well, we care about our families, yours we can spare.

We know that most of you live in the mud and that your lives are full of war and despair, we also know that your life is not going anywhere. Our PR Goddess of control told us to let you think you had a chance to improve, but in reality we rule this game, we know your every move.

Mental and emotional manipulations are cool tools we've learned to use. Hope and a chance of change, we let you think it's in your range. We confuse you and we distract, it's a game we play, and we protect our back.

War, religion, economies, hate, insecurity and fear, we use all these things. We control and we steer. This is our ship, we're in charge and it will stay that way, you will never have a say. You think if you move your pawns across the board you can play? No chance. Your game is lost before it began; we control the life of the common man.

You were told to "Remember, remember…," but you forgot. Okay we had a lot to do with that, we manipulate a lot. The reality is we cannot lose, we have a world to abuse, and we're not finished yet.

Chess, maths, or 'all the world's a stage,' call it anything you like, you can even rage - we don't care - the rules are fixed and we rule over you down there. It's embedded in your long-term education. For a while you were ruled by Kings and Queens but you were slowly coming to understand what that really means - class war. We just monopolised with a new face, we're your masters now - we rule this place: Someone has to, it might as well be us, we move the pawns in this play, we do it very well and we do it every day. Checkmate.

Controlling How Everyone Can Knowingly Mercilessly Attack The Earth

CHESS

Can Humanity Earth Save Somehow

Yes, we understand – for you, it's chess; we understand that for you, life is just a game, something to be won, to increase the power of the player and his name. And mostly we understand that you distract us with new toys, or simply despair. We know you manipulate and you fight for your control, you do it very well, but in a sense, you sold what some people would call your soul.

There is a common goodness that you have lost, it's a sadness that you don't see and feel, your actions are at a high cost; you're blind to this reality. You live in a hall of mirrors where you only see and feel what you project. You the powerful have been embedded to be this way, where you think you must rule and must have the say. Well yes, it's a normal weakness of man, where he thinks he must protect. It's a form of power that's for sure, but anyone can be this negative, you learn that as a child. There's a strange pleasure in a cruelty if it goes a little wild. To seek dominance and control can never leave you whole; it leaves a shadow, a darkness lying on the inner life of man.

It stops you from being a whole Human capable of seeing, and understanding the position of others, to put yourself in their place, to see or feel the suffering upon their face: the death and destruction and endless sorrow that your policies bring today and tomorrow. No, you have no power for this human capacity, you're weak, you've fallen down to the lower level of man, and you protect your position with all you can. The smallest child has more 'Being' than you the 'Powerful Man'. To treat life as a game, that's such a shame. Life is more like a test and you fall down like all the rest - of your kind - you think you are the King and you lead the blind. You are simply a pawn of your lower self and you lead humanity towards this 'Endgame', and yes, in yourself, you are to blame, for not saying No. This is not how it should go.

Being in charge and in power, you could have guided all humanity to a better end than this. You could have – had you been educated to lead humankind, but it's no exaggeration to say, you are the blind, blinded by the attraction of power. You drenched a society in empty sadness, it's not wrong to say this is madness. Yes, we see you call this Chess; you think it's a game. No, that's a mistake, sadly. When organic life dies out, it's a Tragedy. No one wins in this game of control. All of our children die the warming death. With no food or water, no-one's the best. Only the beast in man will be released - at the end. Barbarism has no friends.

Often asked Questions on Global Warming

Some answers are based on now, others at the end of the century, others a little while later.

Global warming – is it real? *Yes.*

Will the seas rise? – *Most definitely.*

Will it get hot? – *As above.*

Will the ice melt? – *Without a doubt.*

Will people survive? – *For a while.*

Will I need suntan lotion? - *Buckets.*

Will my telephone still work? – *There won't be any.*

Will there still be T.V.? – *There won't be any.*

If I have money, will I survive? – *Not for long.*

Why? - *It's predicted that societies will collapse, therefore money will become irrelevant.*

Who will run the world? - *For a while, governments with military control, just the same as it is now, but different. When it's survival, they won't need to hide what and how they do what they do. After that, as the systems fall apart, societies will break up, you can imagine the rest. And either at the same time or soon after it will become just too hot to live. As people can't work outside, there will be no food production and not enough drinkable water. There will be different transition periods, but basically, life as we know it, ceases.*

Can't we live in the ocean? - *Unlikely, it's becoming acidic and we lack the technology. It's more likely that the rich will live partially underground in mountains for a while, but even that's not sure.*

Will we have food? - *Not above a certain temperature.*

Can we move to another planet? - *No, there is no planet 'b' for us.*

What about the films that tell us that may be possible? – *They're just films.*

When will it begin? - *Already has.* - *The programme began at 8 o'clock.*

No, I mean Global Warming. - *Yes, I know, I was just joking.*

Is there any way to stop it? - *No.*

Is there any way to slow it down? - *Yes.*

How? - *Leave the oil, gas, and coal in the ground and switch to renewables immediately; if not today, tomorrow would be good.*

How much time do we have for that? - *Probably between 8 and 15 years. If there's no massive change within that time-frame then the coming heat will be unstoppable.*

When was the last time it was that warm? - *At the end of the Dinosaur age.*

Are they sure it will be that warm again? - *Actually all predictions are said to be on the conservative side, many believe with reasonable cause that it will become much hotter, with unmanageable consequences.*

What makes it different than other times of Global Warming? - *It's said it's the speed that the planet is heating at; it has never heated at this speed before, heating up, was over thousands of years, this is probably due as to how we perceive time. This speed of heating is incredibly fast, our conception of time is limited, we just do not perceive as a reality different time scales. We are small 'Beings', planets are big 'Beings'. After all, we don't call our planet 'Mother Earth' just because it sounds nice.*

Good and bad aspects of Global Warming

Some answers are based on now, others at the end of the century, others a little while later.

On the good side - you won't need to worry about the cold.

On the bad side - it will be too warm to be outside.

On the good side - no need to worry about money.

On the bad side - societies will collapse.

On the good side – no need to vote, no politicians, no government.

On the bad side - there will be repression and dominance by the most violent.

On the good side - no more 9 till 5 boring jobs.

On the bad side - there will be no more society.

On the good side - no need to learn to swim.

On the bad side - you'll die if you go in the water, acid kills.

On the good side - you won't need to worry about being a vegetarian or not.

On the bad side - you'll eat what you can get.

On the good side - no more ten minutes of commercials.

On the bad side - there will be no T.V. and nothing to buy anyway.

On the good side - no need to think about too many people.

On the bad side - people will die out dramatically.

On the good side - there will be no more cars or planes.

On the bad side - no transportation of any sort and in the Hot Hours even walking will be off limits.

On the good side - no need to think about Christmas presents any longer.

On the bad side - it will not exist anymore.

On the good side - no need to worry about people sleeping on the streets.

On the bad side - we will all be in the same boat.

On the good side - we can live off the land.

On the bad side - finding any land that's livable will be difficult.

On the good side - you won't need to read a book like this.

On the bad side - there won't be any books.

On the good side - you won't need to worry about destroying our planet.

On the bad side - it will be too late.

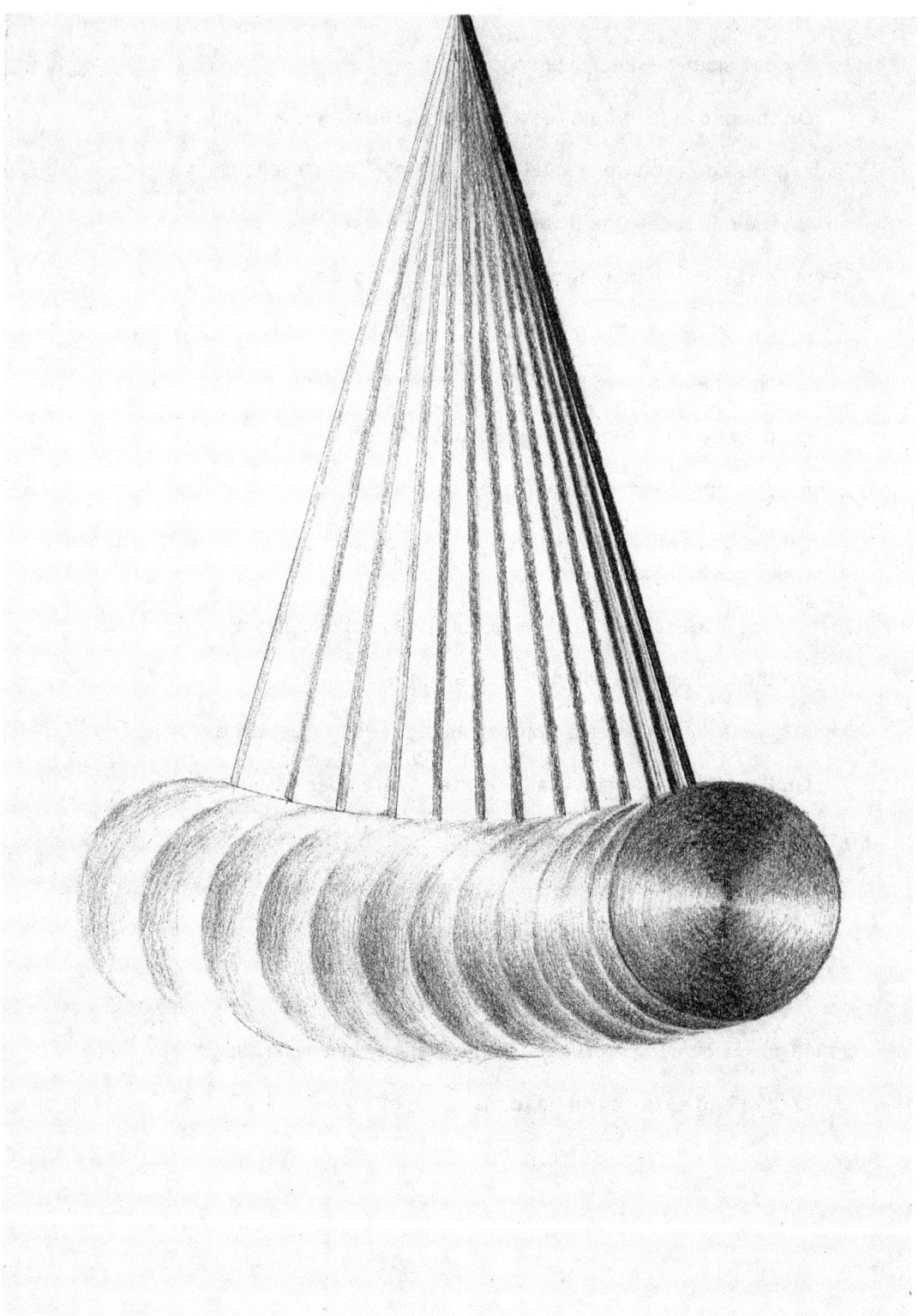

The swing of the pendulum

It was Rosa Luxemburg who said, if we do not go towards socialism we will turn to barbarism instead. A strange statement indeed but she saw something we need. If each thing has its own time and capitalism reaches the full end of its swing, then barbarism is what it will bring.

We have a choice, but not much time, perhaps a generation for world democratic socialism to find. Life for all is not equal, this is clear. The needs that we have may never be near, but we have been told by our leaders of science that our planet is a speeding train and we must stop stoking the fire, from using fossil fuels we must refrain.

A generation to change the way we live. We have so many needs and the rich and powerful are so unwilling to give. The pendulum swings. Social struggles go on through all recorded time; some gains are made and some political games are played, it keeps the masses down below from revolting against what they know - to be a lie. But our needs and aims are now connected; sure, media powers try to leave it undetected. But 99% of scientists say Global Warming is on its way. So not only is our struggle for common rights to bring a balance, but we struggle to keep a planet from going over the edge. It's the greatest challenge.

As the pendulum swings for humanity, barbarism lies at the other side, if we had time maybe another culture would be born, but time is not on our side. Perhaps as people we close our eyes to our predicted future not only because of media manipulation but to the plain fact that if we acknowledged what was wrong we would have to dramatically change our way of life; we are creatures of habit and we love our habits. We're kind of stuck to them: cultivated attitudes, embedded thoughts, whether they are cultural, social, or personal, these are our forget me knots.

There would be so many things to acknowledge and accept; it's difficult: To acknowledge that when you fly other people die. When we continue to support war, countless innocents pay the price. To continue the way of a comfort life you have to stay within your comfort zone, which means not acknowledging certain basic recognized facts which can for a certain time be socially denied or ignored; the main one being that your planet is warming quicker than it should be. If it's not in your face, you don't feel as if you're in a race.

What do we need?

Individual social movements to join together to place pressure on our governments to change society for the benefit of its people and not for the benefit of the ultra-rich. It's nothing new; it's what's been wanted all time through.

Are there any concrete ideas?

Lots, from many sources, here's a few in no particular order. Some might rhyme and some might repeat.

Many movements are everywhere, there are needs and people do care. These needs are different in 'Every-land' but joining them together is what people now understand. The need to stop fracking our lands apart as if doing so is a sacred necessary art. The need for no more oil to be found, the urgent need for it to be left in the ground. The urgent need to listen to all peoples of every land, as it's all of nature that will burn and pay the price for man.

Unions that struggle for more pay, to raise the minimum wage. Ultimately for the workers that work to own the companies they work for in their community. Free transportation within cities would decrease the necessity and wish for cars that would help our planet not looking like Mars. The unemployed to be directed to meaningful work, offering jobs to retrain people in saving our world, and at the same time the workers who have the possibilities to strike, to sit in, slow down or stop the working norm, to let their voice be heard and their actions gain power, not necessarily the battlements to storm.

Also necessary would be a massive conversion to wind and solar energies. Coral reef preservation, implementation of laws and conservation of wildlife everywhere. Also good, would be slowing down the devastation of our oceans. Financing and redirecting the workforce to more helpful food production. Turning food production over to be localized rather than Globalized would be essential for many reasons; cutting out transportation and pesticides and massive land grabs by the already wealthy.

A massive planetary cultivation of the seeding of new trees instead of its opposite would be helpful, kind, and practical. An immediate transformation of how we build our cities, materials, and methods used etc. building against the predicted coming devastations for our kids and theirs.

The struggles against fossil fuel extraction, particularly through mountain top removal and fracking technologies, would be essential as many people now realize.

In general, the stopping and reversing of Austerity measures which negatively affect the poor of every land, which in itself is simply an organized way of going against the laws of gravity, sending money upwards in space towards the already rich.

Ceasing wars of domination which is a multi-headed dragon guarding Pandora's Box. In its massive use of oil, in its extraction of other peoples oil in other lands or under the oceans or the melting ice, which in the end also only feeds monies to the ultra-rich? Added to that and a primary, its countless deaths, devastation, and destruction it brings to millions all over the world.

Taking profit out of war would be good. Taking profit out of fossil fuel extraction we also should. To learn from the indigenous peoples of our planet how they work to have a balance. For governments to stop putting religions at war with each other, we need more educators of tolerance, we need desperately religions to join up in this age, we need bridges of understanding that we and our children must cross, and we need them now.

We need the rich western world to pay for crimes of past times, of slavery, domination, and resource stealing that would enable the poorer countries to develop and respond to climate changes. These are needs to balance our world and it's pretty obvious that our world needs balancing. We need new social rights; we need people of colour freed from gun sights.

We need women more empowered to rule and lead, we need the common human rights that have been trashed and shred, that have been fought for over the last hundred years, rights for which our forefathers have bled. We need these rights back and we need more and we need them now.

We need free education for everyone, free water; it's our planet, 'damn it'. We need to give countries back to the people that live in them. We need to turn the police into a 'people's right' protection force. We need to have leaders that can lead and cannot be bought.

We have many needs but time runs out at high speed, so we need people who have the capacity to think, feel, and empathize, we already know the falseness in politicians eyes, we need to abandon our false gods of greed and self-care, we need new ones for the coming age, we need a society that has sorrow turned into rage. And this must be a change in our age.

Don't we have any of this?

Yes, we do, but social changes are small and often disconnected struggles. The struggles for all the previously mentioned ideas to bring about a more balanced society are happening now, somewhere. But it's like that famous old saying 'divide and conquer'. The rich and powerful controllers know this well. They divide, distract, and deflect attention with multiple methods; then social change stays only the dream, not the reality. Small successes are good and necessary stages, but that gives the illusion of change. The chess pieces are simply being moved around the table a little bit, the (deadly) game goes on.

The end results of these struggles and the powerful attempts to stop or hinder them, means what?

All societies are moving towards totalitarian states either openly or covert, 'Soft deflective power' 'Let them think they are free'. Laws and actions brought into play to control dissent from policy, financial social suffering, less money, no homes, break up the family unit. Imprisonment leads to a cheap workforce and death; they have enough bodies for their needs so it also just maintains a storage of excessive population in public paid-for privatized prisons.

People in general are deflected by inane trivialities, while the house burns down; in other countries simply to survive from bullets and bombs is the daily need. A generation or two of more invented distractions, more embedded or direct control externally will seal humanity's fate. It will seem and be fed to the public as progress, but as the planet heats and the climate changes all over the world, predictions by scientists are - that civilization will fall apart. Food production will slow down and cease, riots and revolutions will occur everywhere, governments will kill their own populations 'en masse' simply to stay in control.

Millions, if not Billions will die in the aftermath of these changes. With no controls in place there will be nothing to stop nuclear weapons from being used, one only has to look at how emotionally volatile and dangerous this attitude is to have that as an option of policy in the first place. As all our societies have different levels and methods of oppression and control, well, for one reason or another civilization will collapse, humanity dies out.

It's not hard to envisage that with no food production all other animals on our planet will be found and killed till there's none left. When we can't plant and grow food, and there will be no animals left, that only leaves each other to eat. Then civilization will have swung to the ultimate end of the pendulum, Barbarism in its most extreme, probably where we started from.

Do you think this could be a wrong point of view to have?

Yes, of course, any attitude strongly held can be wrong if it doesn't consider its opposite, but right or wrong is not the point, it's about time and the chances we take regarding the survival of the human race; we can only consider it from our perception of time, what's happening now and what has happened in the past. All different branches of our science tell us we don't have very long; time runs out for these changes to be made. And if we are not successful soon these are the general predictions for our future, it's not fantasy.

What about the super-rich, can't they help?

Unfortunately they are causing and continuing the problem. It's like people that are addicted to anything; they don't realize that they have a problem and that they make life hell on earth for all others around them. Their own mind set has been adjusted to be that way. They have internalized these weaknesses of human nature, it all seems normal to them. They need self-realization and self-motivation classes to recognize what's wrong and get off the party bus they're on, in short, they need rehab. They are too busy enjoying the negative pleasures and destroying everything else in the process, our rich leaders may be charming, but they are deadly. A little self-mirror shock reality is needed.

That seems like an impossible task.

Yes it does, it's difficult to find a way out of this labyrinth, there are many small answers and solutions, that must eventually all connect up, so let's take one of them from somewhere else. We need the energy of a particular emotion, similar to that contained in the power of sorrow and we need it on a massive scale, that energy of empathy and compassion which in general people only feel in certain moments, under certain circumstances. Not the violent energy of rage and shouting in mass crowds gatherings, that we all know, but the contained energy of a personal awareness of our collected sorrow at this future that we vaguely sense and see coming towards us. That would be extremely difficult, but not impossible.

A sense of the Miraculous

Heroes and all that fairy story stuff

It seems the only way for an alternative ending is for the Hero in each of us to wake and rise to that inner call that whispers gently inside. It is there, in each one of you.

It doesn't speak to you in words; that would be just your mind playing its usual tricks. Words and information are necessary, but only to lead you to the feeling. The hero in you works on your feeling, the feeling of – 'this is wrong'.

But then of course, come the flood of tricks again, when we feel or tell ourselves that we're helpless, just a cog in a machine sort of thing. Never believe that. The Hero is there in you, it's the one that has compassion and empathy for others, human and the non-human species that we share this planet with.

And the Hero in you is talking all the time to your emotion, that's its language, it's emotional. It doesn't need words from any spoken language; that would be confusion, 'the confusion of tongues'. That's why this world movement and emotion to save our planet can become so big. It speaks the universal language of emotion, which as we all know, is in every human: if we listen to it.

It's the language of our conscience, that inner wordless call: we can ignore it and I suppose truth be told, we often do: but we can't get rid of it. We ignore it when we pass the homeless in the street, or perhaps not giving something to those in need or who have less, or ignoring what people in power do in our name. There are so many things we ignore and just get on with life. But that feeling is there, you know it is. It's waiting to be listened to, to help draw the Hero in us upward, to awaken and rise from our slumber that covers us like a veil.

Now I know that all sounds like fairy story sort of stuff, but fairy stories are about all that sort of stuff. Heroes going through difficulties, battles and tests of endurance on their journeys, to eventually awaken not only the sleeping princess, but something in themselves, to find the treasure: and of course the treasure may be something that lies asleep buried deep inside the Hero.

Of course it's all fairy story stuff. But it's the type of stuff that mums and dads for thousands of years tell their young kids, because they still want their kids to believe in a sense of the miraculous, to believe that despite the problems, there's hope: regardless of the difficulties and realities of life, and struggles for survival in the societies we have created on this planet. There is something in us that against all odds, wants to become a real human being with the capacity of empathy and compassion for other beings.

That feeling is not atrophied in humans yet. But it is being attacked mercilessly by behavioural engineered attitudes of patriarchy, racism, bigotry, self-interested violence and power domination tendencies, in destroying something (for lack of a better word) sacred in our kids. By not only allowing but encouraging these attitudes in our kids to develop, initiated by business interests and continued by media control, making billions of profit annually from many of their interconnected projects. These people and yes, it is people, not able to perceive, or ignoring the negative side effects of what they have done and continue to do. They have internalized and now accept that their attitude and thought process on all this is normal, when in fact to any sane thinking person it's abnormal.

Those people are rich and powerful; their inner Hero is on an all-expenses paid permanent holiday and enjoying all the strange pleasures of that power: sadly at the expense of the mass of the population of our world. And it is our world, not theirs, regardless of what they think.

So yes, we are most definitely between 'a rock and a hard place': it's a helluva place to be. And it seems that it's up to each one of us individually, to try to awaken not only ourselves from this surrounding swamp of influences, but to try to help others to recognize our situation, and to attempt collectively to do something about it; for the sake of ourselves, our children and theirs: and in reality, humanity, along with all the other billions of living beings with whom we share our world, who will disappear along with us in the coming onslaught of climate changes from our planet warming quicker than it should be. So yes, between 'a rock and a hard place', just about sums it up. Wanna be a Hero?

> The seeds are sown; this is true;
> it needs anything you can do.
> Turn your voice to this cause,
> we need planetary saving laws.
> Aims that we need to have and hold,
> common movements that must be bold;
> with seeds of hope and seeds of care;
> these movements must grow together everywhere.

> And yes, some have begun,
> this is great, that people walk their talk
> but now the movements must run.
> Wake the Hero that sleeps in you,
> that Hero knows what to do.
> When the Hero does awake,
> the Hero knows what path to take.

Time-Stories

Controllers of Might .com
The Hot Hours
Seeds of Needs

Controllers Of Might .COM

The world was like a Hollywood movie dream. Flying machines were everywhere to be seen, everything worked with Nano-tech high speed. Computers were holograms, or embedded in your eyes. Everything was calculated, for life, there was no surprise.

It followed a principle that was discovered, that anything you could think of could be covered, all it took was a little time, and everything you thought was made fine. There was just one problem that did appear, it was the companies that controlled all that was near, everything was now embedded and with a chip - you were wedded.

It was given to you at birth; it was just like all the movies told it would be. The company lived inside you silently. Nowhere could you go without being traced, there were cameras everywhere: modern man - a recorded face. If you were nervous to a high degree, you were monitored silently. With the power of the Gods your heartbeat could be read, all to predict what went through your head. Dissent was a thing of the past, independent thought could never last.

All must have food these days; the silencing drugs were supplied these ways. Just a touch was all that was needed and the urge to comply was truly seeded, genetic manipulation grew into the highest form of art, once you were embedded, dissent was silenced from the start. For controllers of might it was always the same, control over mankind was the aim of the game.

There were those that tried to dissent and fight against the company machine, but it was as if fighting in a dream, it changed all the time. And a dream was the right way to think about it, for the company of might controlled it all. They believed in a God that all must follow; all must dream the dream and their faith must always be seen.

The police were the holy followers, the protectors of the day. In warming times these were their ways, and they shall follow them till the end of days. The oil almost gone, so they turned to solar to keep control, to make their energies - to keep the company whole.

The oceans rise now upon the lands, men now retreat to higher grounds, and are building cities deep in the ground. We build there now because we must, our God did tell us, 'we build or bust'.

The poor and slaves of the world dig long and deep 24-7-365 to prepare and maintain the 'holy hive', where all shall live and work and die from the heat death coming bye. Parts of the world now rebel and many people begin to speak and tell of the injustices they endure, and the laws that keep them poor; they rise in protest and they fight against the 'Controllers Of Might'.

The internet of olden times is no longer the peoples' dream; all is under the control of one. They said it was better to succumb. The world must go the way it must; we all believe in one God to pray, their one system, he wants this way '.COM' is the name for one and all. Controllers of might, what else could it be; '.com' can all things see. He knows your every wish and desire, he sees you in every moment of every day, 24-7-365, he's a God who never goes away.

24-7-365, a God that never sleeps, and who controls everything; he tells us he wants the world to heat, for to live in mountains will be a treat. He wants us to burn all the oil we find, gas and minerals are good for your body and your mind. Now everyone must bow down to the greater cause, our God has made these laws. You will be happy to be a cog in the machine, this is life and we live a dream. The animals all die out, but God wants that to, he wants the planet just for you; you will multiply and you will spread, you're never alone not even in your bed.

We need workers to dig in deep, and when they die, their secrets keep, a population kept on drugs, some to increase their strength for working every day with a built in side effect of a 'EOL' expediency; but that's okay, we have 'mother bees', we breed your seeds as we please; and you are educated from the moment you are born. We embed it all in your chip, if we want to we can make you trip. A population kept under control, we subdue you to keep you whole, love our God - '.COM'.

He's been waiting for you all along, we've been working in the dark, so you couldn't see us light the spark, but generally we distract and attract you, we gave you lots of toys, hell – we thought you knew. You can always rely on the weaknesses and mentality of man, we should know, we kept you uneducated and living down below. We turned you back to slavery with a little freedom for pleasure, but it's calculated 'measure for measure'. We found a balance for humankind. The 1% see - the 99% are blind. We really like it that way, how we control you every day.

Their last instruction before the wars: we have enough to breed, kill all the others we don't need.

The Hot Hours

After the wars

She looked out from the safety of the cave over the mostly barren land. She had lived all her short life here, as probably most of the others did who lived on this mountain. Her family had moved here as the devastation became worse, they had tried several other places, but eventually stayed here.

Her mum and dad said it was the safest place they had found. They needed the cave; it wasn't possible to be out in the burning sun during the Hot Hours, that's when everyone rested, as they were doing now. So she could be alone and looking out over the land. She had to stay sitting in the shade otherwise the direct heat would burn her. No-one could survive outside in the Heat, in the Hot Hours of the day.

The evenings were wonderfully warm, always; even the inside of the cave was never cold. There had been a couple of days where she had felt the cold, her father had said he didn't know why, it just was that way sometimes. But he had only felt that a few times in his life.

Her father told her that possibly in some parts of the world people still lived in large mountain cities: with machines that controlled the Heat, they had prepared them over the last hundred years. He said the people who were forced to build those mountain cities where called the 'slaves to the machine'. And it was the machines that caused the Heat, but then he said, that wasn't true exactly. The men who had used the machines used black liquid from the Earth. They took it out with machines, that fed other machines and that it was a vicious circle that humans couldn't stop. They built those cities by using the black liquid.

He also said, there used to be billions of people all over the world: many lived near the coast, like his great grandmother used to. She had lived on the coast when the power storms started to increase and the devastations came again and again. A long time ago it was once a year and in different places. Now, they came many times all year round, stronger and stronger.

She could see them from the mountain when they passed across the land, for when they came towards the mountain; they put the protection doors over. They had small windows of the 'unbreakable glass' saved from older times. But she felt lucky; from where they lived they could always see the beautiful 'Sky-art'.

The only real problems were getting enough food and the 'slave-eaters', the robbers who killed; they travelled across the land. Of course they didn't travel in the Hot Hours, but that still left them several hours every-day. They needed to rest in protected areas, so that slowed them down. Her father said as the animals died out the slave-eaters hunted people and they were the real danger now and they had weapons. They hunted for people, for meat, and slaves; it had been that way for a long time now.

They could live in their mountain for many years if it wasn't for the 'slave-eaters'. Most of the time there was always someone on lookout over the land, except in the Hot Hours, but even then she often looked out herself or with a friend.

Over time the paths up had been protected; there were weapons and traps in place, that would hold back an attack, for a while, but their defenses were not impenetrable. They had food supplies but it would never be enough for survival, they all feared the slave-eaters, they followed other ways, evil ways.

Her people still had ancient things from the times before the Heat, but most didn't work anymore. There was a time of complete chaos over the world, with much destroyed. Billions died.

The 'Controllers Of Might' had turned their flying weapons on the people. The stories they told in the evenings explained their history. Some things sounded wonderful, it seemed as if it was another planet. She really couldn't believe that 150 years ago, people lived like that and travelled in machines, even in the air, and hundreds all in the same machine, it must have been a big machine. She had never seen even fifty people.

Her father told her that they can only live in caves now. On the lands there was no protection, and there would be even less food to find if they travelled and the water was not always drinkable. He said all of the good caves were occupied now by small groups, if there were enough survivors from the wars, but they had no way of knowing that for sure.

It was difficult to trust any who travelled over the land, they could be scouts for slavers, checking out the terrain, so these days no-one was trusted. Too many mistakes were made in the past.

Slavers were very good at pretending they were 'Travellers'. All they had to do was stay quiet and not talk too much, silence was their disguise, and once they gained your confidence and found where you dwelled, they would leave after a while, then they'd return with a much larger band. That was their way of getting food and slaves: an evil way.

Her father had told her several times of late, that it was hotter now than any time before. It may be that our time here will be over soon; that it could change from one day to the next. We must be aware of living and of life while we can. This planet will lose this thing called man.

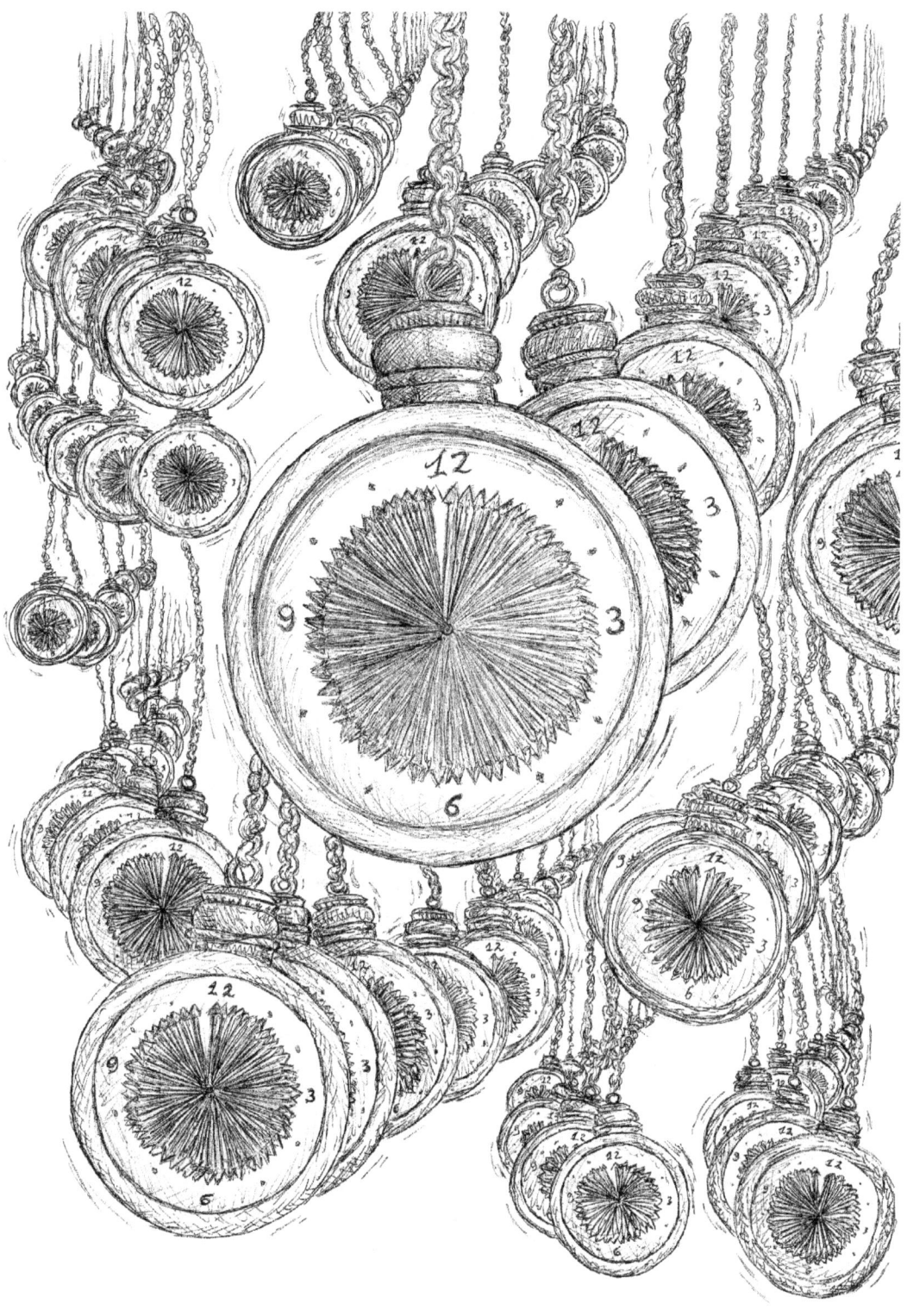

A different future of time

Seeds of Needs

The Urgency of Now - in an Age of Change

Opening speech of a social history class

Some things seem to run in cycles, like the pendulum swings from one side to the other. Well, now it was the women's turn to take power, to rise, to lead the human race away from its deadly face. The mothers of our planet rose to this call – all for one and one for all.

A social state of consciousness of the human fate became the key, people voted into office those in the left of society, those countries that still had the power to vote and choose, leaders that would take another path, this would start a chain reaction in its aftermath.

In the past this was handled by the 'controllers of might', they used their power against the poor to fight, and in many countries of the world it was a one way thing. Death and destruction was the song they did sing. They had a Goddess called TINA; there is no alternative once you've seen her. The controllers loved her and they did comply, their life was sold to live the lie. But then the people became informed about those that .com stormed. The people of the world began to see that this was not how the world should be. A social society is our need, for a warming planet we must heed.

In half the world the voting system could be used, in the other half women were still abused; but as they became the leaders in countries of wealth and power; deals were made - other women in other lands they did empower. Their call was simple in the main, no longer is this world man's sole domain.

There was work that had to be done, no longer did women succumb. Only through the power of the females of the human race could the necessary emotions be unleashed and harnessed for a Global good. They changed all societies that they could. No more patriarchy, no more racism, no more abuse, equality for all. Correct the danger done to planet Earth – before the ultimate fall.

The laws were changed. It was a while in the making, but time no more could they be forsaking. Oil was left in the ground, no more was to be found. Armies were guided and turned to other works. No more invasions of other countries, there was now a real responsibility to protect – our planet.

Education was the main tool of transformation; older women took care of all, they were returned to this necessary call, to become teachers of the new rules and laws, this became for many their true cause. Education as a tool, it was clear that men lacked something in their history of domination and control. Time was running out, a heating planet left the world in no doubt. One generation to make the planet whole.

All the teachings that people followed in the times of the 'Age of Change', were gathered together, men no longer ruled the range. The hierarchy of these structures transformed like a fairy story, for it was clear we lose our world and all we hold dear, unless women were allowed to be in control and steer - all humanity on a new path. Death companies were disbanded in the aftermath.

This now was the call for all to do, to lead our planet to something new – an Age of Change – of transformation of our ways that had led us to these warming days. This had to be a change for all; it was humanity's last call. For that to work it had to be personal and collective, from the ways we had followed we had to be selective: we drew from the sources the best we could. We transformed the world – now all had food. An equal pay was had for all, there was no lower down to fall. If you owned a house that was okay, taxes were made accordingly.

Controllers of care

As to policing and keeping order in the streets, well, now they were all common places to meet. For many years the main policy and function of the police was to protect the interests of the rich; with their laws to be overseen, sadly, the police had been militarized, what it was is not how it should have been.

The rich had been safe in their towers of wealth, it was the poor in reality that had been policed, of course many took their work to a high order of respect. But in some others that was hard to detect, demilitarized, and transformed back into something that became the norm.

The justice system was re-managed; laws were changed for it was damaged. A restructuring of society from top to down, from bottom to up, a social common goodness sense was the answer to our defense, of the 'Age of Change'.

Everyone had meaning and worth

The unemployed were sent to work in all manner of ways. The riches of the oil wealth were taken and redirected, that conjoined with all the money spent on war. We had enough for all our plans, we turned them into law.

The death companies of war were disbanded, any complaints and they were left stranded; there was no argument to make, our planet Earth was at stake. They could keep some wealth and live well, but that was it, no more death did they sell.

Education and food for all every day, women placed in positions of power over all, no-one could make profit from anything, M-C-M was being transformed, we had another social norm. Millions were re-educated and set to work; solar power, wind and water were all enabled. With women in charge, the world was stabled.

Trees were planted in their millions and all the world over, deals were made to transition the petro states in need. An exchange of commodities was just the common coin, no more useless products were to be made, products were made to last longer so waste would decline. Atomics were simply banned and brought to a regulated end – no arguments on them were ever to depend.

Surveillance of all society was ceased, privacy laws were increased. No more were the elite of old in charge, the internet was set free, basically, how it was meant to be.

Of course for a while a degree of control was maintained to allow our changes to be implemented and the time needed for our changes to be seeded. The movement of the Age of Change was strong, to bring the world back to where it should belong.

There were counter revolutions against our changes and demands, but they were not as strong as the power at our command. We became the new power and social media - we did control. We controlled the boycotts in the beginning; that we placed everywhere. No more profit was to be made unless they were policies of care. Our seeds were sown everywhere.

We had policies of social equality and care, we no longer left it to chance, that form of history was old romance. We became the new and the power of change.

From the beginning, the class system began to transform; an experiment for the common good: there were many in the making. Each country had its different parties partaking in common social laws. They, over time were joined as a band, for no longer must they fight old laws of their land.

The future was coming and it was plain to see that it would be Hot and no more the human race would be. If we had not acted in our days, then before the end of times it would have been billions dead of barbarous ways. Production would slow and stop; the rule of law would break and drop.

Killing would be a common; man would fall down to the lowest state; as the waters rose only understanding would abate. It wouldn't even follow the paths of old cultures after the last decline. With all the animals dead and gone and too hot to be in the sun, mankind would live in the dark and on human flesh feast. Man returns back to the beast. This was the fate of humankind, had the 'Age of Change' not arisen and changed our mind.

Our understanding was awoken; our inner voice had softly spoken. Women, the caring nurturing side of the human race, took charge of the human path, "It's almost too late - but there is a way - if women take over and seize the day. World compassion must begin to grow; a world education must begin to sow – the seeds of change." Those were the words said, as the transforming laws were read.

The restructuring of cities became a common work for many, social works implemented, transportation became free, and cities restructured at last, cars basically became a thing of the past. Speed rail moved with solar, travelled like the wind from head to tail.

Meat production began to drop; soon the whole industry was transformed. We took the world on a difficult path, we planned for the future, but not just the near, the now, and the enduring. We built cities connected to deep in our mountains; their construction was all over the world. Super domes strong enough to withstand the power of the coming storms, we planned for the future well.

Everywhere there was a cultivation of food, for all people now something was good. Windmills were built all over the lands of storm. Solar installed everywhere it was now the norm. Everything that needed to be changed was seeded. It all adapted to necessity of time and place. But it was a warming world and we were in a race.

Those who these movements led, changed their roles, so no-one stayed in place and control, it was part of our movement that made us a unique whole - one for all and all for one.

It would take hours to tell you of the changes we made, but our people became Heroes, no longer enslaved. We needed the power to make a change and that power had always been in range, it was near, never far away, it was women that must rule the day.

In general men had been corrupted through time, it was in their psychology and it was clear it would never change, of course at first this idea was strange, but they were leading the world back to the age of the beast, for if society fell, as it would, the beast would be released.

Men abused their positions of power and control, they had no moral center that was whole, not for all of course, this was not the case, but for those in power, this was their face. We needed a world of Heroes to rise against the injustices that came from their lies, the common people took their cue from the countries where the indigenous were still in contact with the land they knew.

They insisted we care for Mother Earth and made laws for her to protect. The people of the world began to suspect – the truth. That their society was heading out of control and slaving populations, body and soul, people treated like pieces of meat, people forced to sleep in the street, education was being trashed, but the rich were being unmasked.

They had guns and media for control and populations were becoming incarcerated whole, being turned into a world of slave camps, those still in the streets observed from street lamps. Control was becoming total, everyone had a phone embedded with a GPS chip, you were never alone, they could even switch it on and listen to what you say everywhere, any day.

Access to anything that you wrote or said, it was made a social game, one big family all the same, control was total in the main, behavioural engineering was a really cool game. People directed to accept anything into their life that crept.

So yes, Heroes were needed to rise, to wake, to stop the speeding train and put on the brake. It began; it took a while, this social change in the life of humankind. The emotional capacity of women was empowered to lead, to break the chains and seed our common needs. Being the mothers of our race, they had a quality that men could not keep apace. They led the way for new days in the 'Age of Change'. All social movements joined together, after all it was 99% of humanity, thus we were called the 99, we changed the world – we occupied it. Thank you for this chance to explain in the first of these social history classes of the 99 and their Heroes. One of you will be the speaker in the next of these classes. I look forward to listening to you all.

Epilogue

I Am You

I am the Tiger you have made extinct.
I am the Gorilla you so despise,
for you see a mirror in my eyes.
I am the Fish in the ocean, the ocean of emotion,
you so wantonly destroy.
I am the Dolphin, and I am like you,
with nothing to eat we die too.
I am the Horse, and there will be nowhere left to run,
you can't run in the burning sun.
We too will die out, this you will find out.
We are the Sheep that for clothing and meat
you do shear
and we too will die out there.

I am your Dog, your Cat and we must leave with you.
I am the Cattle that you do so breed to slaughter.
I am the Earth, your mother and your daughter.

I am the great Whale, but I too shall die, because our
oceans become acidic from the poisons in the sky.
I am the Bird that no longer will fly.
I am the Elephant, we feel and we think,
but we have nothing left to drink.
I am the Trees, the lungs of your life,
many of us live 1000 years, if you leave us alone,
when we disappear, there will be no life.

I am the disappearing Ice.
I am the Water that will come in the floods.
I am the Lightning that has many times multiplied.
I am the Heat that comes with the fire
and believe me; your life will become dire.

I am the Rain, that the like, you have never seen before
and I will fall heavily upon your door.

I am the Tsunami, the Tornado, the Hurricane,
we will return stronger, again and again.
I am the Poor, a billion in dire need
and we cry out, but you do not heed.
I am the Rich, I will burn as well
and I will see you all in hell.
I am the Desert, and will cover all things.
I am the snow which will give you a beautiful glow.
I am the transformer in your food chain.
I am the Nature that will burn.
I am and I will die and not return,
not in your lifetime.

I am Hope, and am running away, I can't exist when it
gets hotter every day, pretty soon I will be gone, try to
make a collective wish and I'll come along.

I am the People, who realize nothing of what we do,
our eyes are open, but we're blind,
for I am lost and you must find.
I am all Nature and I do cry, so much life, just to die.
I am the Planet and I do weep too,
for I lose a part of me, that's you.

I am the Sun; the Earth is my child,
human beings have been sadly rather wild.
but you are a part of me too, for I lie deep within you.
The spark for your life is given from me
and that can never die.
It will return to its home, that is I
for 'I am' and can never be otherwise,
for the real never ceases to be
your essence returns to me.
I am you
You are me
I am

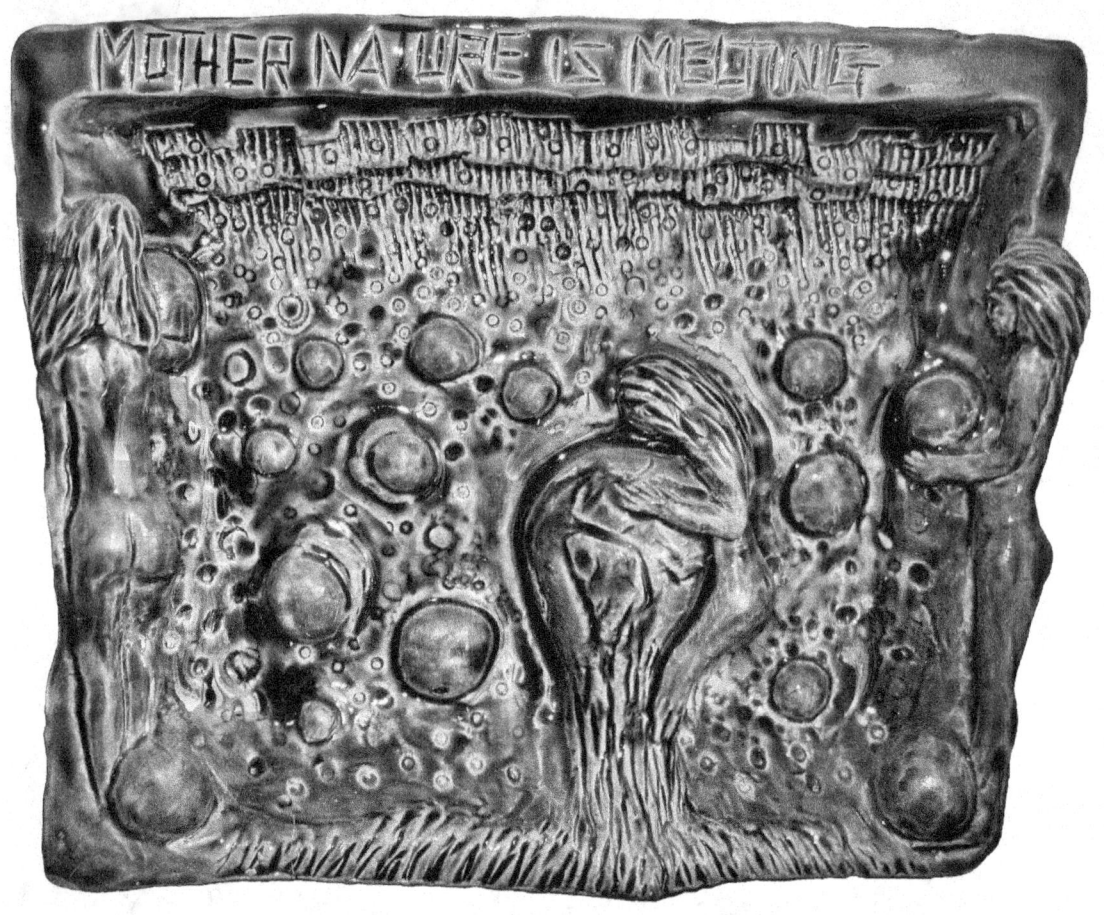

Weather Tales

Rain

Rain dropped and spoke to the water as it sank;
we're dropping now, we carry pain;
we have poisons for your deep domain;
humans caused it; to nature it's a sin.
We're sorry, but we must now give it to you,
you know what you must do.

Sea

We're sad that we lose all life; it's a tragedy that did befall;
now there's no way to change it all.
We will take it because we know we must;
we know it changes all within, much will die,
it won't take long;
and all life will go back to where it came from.
As these poisons sink into me, acid it will turn to be.
Most of life is dead and gone,
for the rest it won't take long.

Wind

We come strong upon the sea;
we have to, the world is heating, it's how it has to be.
We feel it now and how it must be so:
here come the storms that you don't know.

Long ago in times past we were this strong, nothing did last:
we cause you the sea to rise and move;
they call us a Hurricane, but we have a groove:
a space, a place of quiet within the eye of our storm,
peace lives there but not for long.

We move and travel across the sea,
but we seek towards land and somewhere else to be.
Between the storm and the sea, nothing is left.
We don't look on it as destruction;
it's just from nature a little instruction:
For things must change to survive.
It will take a few human years, but for us, we have no fears,
we are simply nature's path; things change in the aftermath.

Heat

Heat was coming more every day,
it spoke to nature and said it was time to change its way.
We need you to adjust, it's not a request, it's a must.
Heat always had the last word, for in the silence of the universe
only heat was ever heard. Heat being one of the energies of the Sun,
a burning furnace that is impossible to know from life down below.

We belong to this small piece of land,
there's no way we can understand.
We move, we travel, we're never still,
it wasn't us that made our planet ill.
That was the experiment called 'the wise man',
it won't be repeated, come back, he never can.

Nature

For nature to fulfil its role, a balance must be there for it to be whole. A pendulum swings till the opposite it brings. A balancing of tensions supports all the strings, so that together a note may be struck; this has nothing to do with chance or luck.

Nature must bring the balance back itself, it surrounds a planet; it needs to look after its health. It's a beautiful barrier of life between 'a rock and a hard place'. Humans are only a tiny part of all species that live on this little planet of natural art, out here in the extremity of space; somehow they thought they were the universal face.

Like a farmer that ploughs through the home of ants,
to them, it's a disaster with which they must deal.
To the farmer he's just organizing with his plough,
he needs to care for the land somehow,
so that he may sow the seeds for a new life:
so, nature's just a farmer taking care of human strife.

25,000 Years...No more the time of tears

Universal contemplation - a gathering of Beings

A lonely Planet out in space, life left this once busy place. The heat scorched all that was left above the sea, that wasn't much compared to what it used to be. It is a water planet now, and for a while it will stay that way, mostly life, just died away.

That planet had been poisoned from within and without; the last human species had no real clue to what real life was about. They were special in their way, but they only stayed for a few 'Earth Days.' Not long at all really, and for the Sun, only moments did they flicker and burn. An experiment, failed, another would begin, but it will be different now, humans won't be tried again, mistakes were never repeated in this universe of change.

The vastness of the ocean is the key to where life will be, the Earth is not finished yet on its journey; at some point, it will bring nature back, once it's recovered from this human attack - upon its health - Earth wants nature to come again to supply what it needs; there will be a cultivation of many different new seeds – of life. It needs this transforming barrier between itself and the universe if it's to continue on its path of growth and change, but it doesn't need man - that experiment was strange.

It was strange that mostly they didn't guess that the universe was inside them, and they only had to look, sense, and see, granted that's how they had to be, continuously blind. They were given help regularly all through their time, but due to unfortunate conditions, distorted it became; mostly they just killed each other in their God's name, and their God had different names: that really was strange.

This gathering of 'Beings', 'God's helpers' shed no tears, have no fears; they answer to another call. They see and understand a different universe of all. They have no religion to behold, only a God to be told. One or all, it's the same; everywhere, in every name, penetrating all 'Being' to the core, it was only a lack of seeing that caused humans this to ignore.

See, sense, become aware, he's looking for you everywhere, for he is you, and you, you cannot leave, it makes no difference what you believe. It's as above and so below, as well, within as without, mostly humans didn't find this out. They discovered a little, but nothing really new – and at their end they were faced with a question, what on Earth did you do?

The wheel turns countless times. Eternity cannot be comprehended, there's always something to be mended. The point becomes the line, becomes the circle of time, never breaking nor completing but always at the same place of meeting, ever to repeat. Time turns into itself, this is ever-last. 'The unreal has no being – the real never ceases to be.'

God's helpers silently understood and accepted, contemplation time was over; they had lots of other things to do for the Creator. Even for them, Time was limited.

www.ingramcontent.com/pod-product-compliance
Lightning Source LLC
Chambersburg PA
CBHW081353280526
45788CB00009B/2865